"In *The Next Worship*, Sandra prov~~ides competent insight and practical~~ advice for ministry leaders seeking to present a more credible witness of God's love for all people in an increasingly diverse and cynical society."
Mark DeYmaz, author of *Building a Healthy Multi-ethnic Church* and *re:MIX*

"The *Next Worship* reminds us that unity is not about uniformity, but about harmonizing rather than homogenizing. Van Opstal reminds us that what may be just as important as how we worship is who we worship with. This is a beautiful book."
Shane Claiborne, author and activist, codirector, Red Letter Christians

"For those of us who are committed to the work of Christian community development in vulnerable neighborhoods, being rooted in a faith community with an expression of worship that is rooted in our struggle for justice and reconciliation is essential. Sandra's new book, *The Next Worship*, provides a much needed resource for leaders who are committed to crafting worship experiences rooted in diversity."
Noel Castellanos, CEO and president, CCDA

"This book is insightful, practical, immensely helpful and profound! Van Opstal blends an academic understanding of peoples and cultures, with a pastor's heart, and a practitioner's no-nonsense advice. Many claim to value multiethnic worship, but few have journeyed so deeply, and so broadly—Van Opstal is one of those few."
Nikki Toyama-Szeto, vice president, Global Church Strategies, International Justice Mission

"This book addresses our spiritual mandate for inclusion and also provides very practical tools, stories and examples from which the reader is able to gain incredible insight, avoid common crosscultural pitfalls, and acquire an increased sensitivity and awareness. I recommend this book not only to anyone seeking to understand and develop multiethnic worship communities, but also to anyone seeking to understand God's heart for diversity and how to engage our neighbors more meaningfully."
Mark Reddy, executive producer, The Justice Conference

"This immensely practical volume also provides hope and how-to advice for preparing (sometimes reluctant) congregations to worship in ways that connect them with the global church in their community and abroad. In a refreshingly broad approach, Sandra Van Opstal goes beyond discussions of music styles to explore what multiethnic worship might look like in Scripture reading, prayers, other arts, the Lord's Supper, the teaching of the Word and more."
Robin P. Harris, president, International Council of Ethnodoxologists

"Weaving theological, intercultural and practical insights, *The Next Worship* presents readers with needed wisdom, enabling us to see the challenges we face as well as the faithful steps we must take. This is a valuable resource for anyone who is engaged in the ministry of worship, indeed the ministry of the gospel, in today's divided, multicultural world."
Peter Cha, associate professor of pastoral theology, Trinity Evangelical Divinity School

"We need to figure out today how to worship across the vast diversity of the church, with a particular attentiveness to those voices on the margins. With rich biblical reflection and vivid examples from decades of experience at the intersection of racial reconciliation and worship, my friend Sandra Van Opstal has written a definitive resource for the church today."

Matthew Soerens, US church training specialist, World Relief, coauthor, *Welcoming the Stranger*

"Van Opstal calls worship leaders to be anthropologists as well as theologians: self-aware students of culture who engage in critical reflection about their contexts, who take responsibility for interpreting their actions and who summon the courage and humility to truly collaborate."

Monique Ingalls, professor of church music, Baylor University

"We tend to be captivated by our own voice, yet worship in heaven joyfully incorporates the rich voices of people from all cultures and nations. Sandra offers us a field guide, or training manual to prepare us now for the wondrous diversity of heaven's worship."

Tim Dearborn, director, Lloyd John Ogilvie Institute of Preaching, Fuller Theological Seminary

"Sandra Van Opstal takes us on a journey through different multicultural worship experiences and helps us learn valuable lessons from them. Van Opstal's work beautifully builds on my early observations about the power of multicultural worship to bring together the diverse people of God."

George Yancey, author of *Beyond Racial Gridlock* and *Hostile Environment*

"Van Opstal moves us to stand with our diverse congregations in postures of hospitality ('we welcome you'), solidarity ('we stand with you') and mutuality ('we need you'). Van Opstal skillfully guides us through processes of change, the necessity of shared leadership and the challenges and joys of training other leaders for this task."

Steven C. Roy, associate professor of pastoral theology, Trinity Evangelical Divinity School

"This book—rooted in the biblical theological understanding of servanthood—is vital to facilitating worship in any context. Regardless of where you are on the journey, this book encourages, challenges and convicts you to model the kingdom in the way Christ models it for us!"

Stephen Kelly, worship leader, Willow Creek Chicago, worship arts director, North Park University

"If we worship leaders are taking our pastoral roles seriously, one of our jobs is to prepare our churches for heaven's worship where all nations are gathered. This book inspires, encourages and teaches how to do just that!"

Zac Hicks, pastor of worship, Coral Ridge Presbyterian Church, author of *The Worship Pastor*

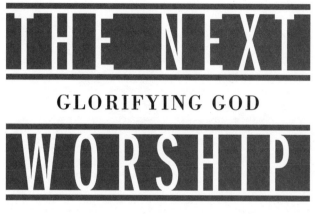

THE NEXT

GLORIFYING GOD

WORSHIP

IN A DIVERSE WORLD

Sandra Maria Van Opstal

foreword by Mark Labberton

IVP Books

An imprint of InterVarsity Press
Downers Grove, Illinois

InterVarsity Press
P.O. Box 1400, Downers Grove, IL 60515-1426
ivpress.com
email@ivpress.com

InterVarsity Press® is the book-publishing division of InterVarsity Christian Fellowship/USA®, a movement of students and faculty active on campus at hundreds of universities, colleges and schools of nursing in the United States of America, and a member movement of the International Fellowship of Evangelical Students. For information about local and regional activities, visit intervarsity.org.

While any stories in this book are true, some names and identifying information may have been changed to protect the privacy of individuals.

Cover design: David Fassett
Interior design: Beth McGill
Images: © 501room/iStockphoto

ISBN 978-0-8308-4129-5 (print)
ISBN 978-0-8308-9948-7 (digital)

Printed in the United States of America ∞

Library of Congress Cataloging-in-Publication Data
Names: Van Opstal, Sandra, 1974-
Title: The next worship : glorifying God in a diverse world / Sandra Maria
  Van Opstal ; foreword by Mark Labberton.
Description: Downers Grove : InterVarsity Press, 2015. | Includes
  bibliographical references and index.
Identifiers: LCCN 2015036030 | ISBN 9780830841295 (pbk. : alk. paper)
Classification: LCC BV15 .V353 2015 | DDC 264—dc23
LC record available at http://lccn.loc.gov/2015036030

P	23	22	21	20	19	18	17	16	15	14	13	12	11	10	9	8	7	6	5	4
Y	34	33	32	31	30	29	28	27	26	25	24	23	22	21	20	19	18	17			

CONTENTS

FOREWORD

by Mark Labberton

Everything turns on worship. Living in the light of the love of the triune God is supposed to be our human vocation. Our very life is made for this purpose, and all our energies are best discovered and unleashed when we see them in this context and for this purpose. A full vision of worship encompasses every dimension of life: our family, our jobs, our friendships, our questions, our suffering, our sin, our recreation, our imagination, our play, and our dying and death.

Worship actively places us before the true and living God and calls us to respond with every dimension of who we are. Faithful worship unlocks and opens, calls and guides us in our life as faithful exiles. As we live lives of worship, we bear witness to the grace of God that enlarges our hearts and minds and extends our capacities to love and serve. We are a people called to a peculiar life.

All of this means worship should be fundamentally disruptive. If our experiences of worship, particularly corporate worship, are doing their work, they will draw us *toward* our God of forgiving, transforming love, even as they draw us *away* from lives of absorbing self-interest and preoccupation. As those who know we are to "seek first the kingdom of God," we gradually abandon the kingdom of self. The evidence of this transformative process is that our neighbor—no "mere" mortal, as C. S. Lewis says—becomes ever more vividly and consequentially present and urgent in our lives. So it would be impossible to say we "love God" and "not love our neighbor." Faithful worship inevitably leads us to this and makes this dual reality plain.

What Sandra Van Opstal does so importantly here is to help make the arc of this worship transformation clear and practicable. Out of her life experience and rich ministry background, Sandra does for us here what she has done over the years for many of those she has led as worship teams and as worshipers. This book is a vital gift for a changing church that needs to reflect the God of all the nations.

As our neighbors change, our worship needs to change. If our worship does not include or embody our love for our real neighbors, then it does not adequately reflect the God we worship. Now, and in the coming decades, the worship we offer will be done amidst a world of teeming variation of people and places. This multicultural worship is not about politically correct decorative variation, but about profound incarnational faith.

To this end, Sandra has written as a wise, experienced and nuanced practitioner. She knows what she is writing about and she is convinced—as am I—that multicultural worship is critical for our theology, and for our mission. Sandra is pointing to what is compelling and urgent because it is worship that draws us toward God and toward our neighbor. This is not easy. It has always been, however, the call of the church that is to be a reflection of the heart of God who "so loved the world that he gave us his only begotten son."

ACKNOWLEDGMENTS

Our thoughts and practices are developed in community! This work is as much a work of the dozens of teams of musicians, pastors and students that I have collaborated with as it is mine. Thank you, InterVarsity staff and students, for allowing me to spend almost two decades experimenting. I especially appreciate the partnership of the Urbana 03, 09 and 12 teams. Thank you, Melissa Vallejo, Andy Kim, Ryan Cook and Erna Hackett, for the stimulating conversations about worship, culture, leadership and food. Thanks to mentors who have championed me: Brenda Salter McNeil, Rick Richardson, Peter Cha, Mark Labberton, Steve Roy and Orlando Crespo. Thanks to John Witvliet of the Calvin Institute of Christian Worship and Robin Harris of the International Council of Ethnodoxologists for allowing me to test my ideas and for the invaluable resources and feedback.

Special thanks to my family. To my parents, Miguel and Olga, and my siblings, Erica, Sofia, Omar, Libby, Alan and Beth, for supporting me and helping me to keep it real. To my church, Grace and Peace, for giving me space, encouragement and prayer to finally finish. To my husband, Karl, for participating at just about every worship session, transcribing the many café conversations I had with leaders and pastors, and editing every version of this book that existed. You forced me to finish this book, reminding me along the way that I can always blog new material and thoughts by chanting "We must have closure!"

I dedicate this book to my son, Justo Alejandro Ostroski, who embodies in his name the reality of the future of the church and the call for us to live justly!

INTRODUCTION

What does worship look like for a college student movement seeking to reach out to the campus in all of its ethnic diversity? What might it look like on their campuses, at their leadership training camps or when they gather thousands of students to mobilize them for global mission? To get an idea, let's first take a look back.

At InterVarsity's earliest Urbana Student Missions Conferences in the 1940s and 50s, worship reflected both the student population at the gathering as well as the churches they attended: organ, piano and choir. As the years passed, InterVarsity Christian Fellowship USA and InterVarsity Canada, the hosting organizations of Urbana, saw the opportunity and embraced the challenge of adapting the worship to reflect the changes in our North American context. Historically, music had been led with a piano on one corner of the platform, organ on the other and the worship leader at the middle. Music at Urbana was sung from a hymnal; primary hymns, and later black spirituals and short choruses were sung.

A shift occurred in 1970, when the worship leadership moved from being a white male to an African Canadian, who led until 1987. Then in 1990 a band was introduced, which was composed of a multiethnic team, but led by a white male. There were many stakeholders in this transition, and change is always hard. As Alison Siewert, performing arts director for Urbana 15, reflected on that era she said, "It was messy, incomplete, and fraught—it was funny to think back about how many swamps we had to wade through and to be grateful again that Jesus got us through them."[1]

Urbana 93 brought a significant change with the introduction of shared leadership. Using ethnically diverse leadership of both women and men allowed each to fully utilize his or her gifts. One leader was gifted at pastoral direction for congregations, another excelled in arranging music and a third was passionate about developing leaders on the team. In 1996 these same leaders were able to put processes and structures in place that set the foundation for worship teams that followed. They also expanded the selection of global music, using a few foreign-language songs, but the default was the dominant culture. They also recorded a live CD to be used as a training tool for the movement. Every decade brought significant transition that affected both the conference and InterVarsity's worship culture across the movement.

Dr. Monique Ingalls, an ethnomusicologist and professor at Baylor University, describes Urbana as "earthly rehearsals for the heavenly choir" in her study on how our worship shapes our understanding of what is to come.

On the opening night of the triennial Urbana (Missions) conference on December 27, 2006, I sit in the midst of an excited crowd of an estimated 23,000 college students gathered in St. Louis' Edward Jones Dome. Attendees stream into the stadium, filling the sloping bleachers on three sides of the dome which face a wide front stage. The gathered participants cheer loudly when the twelve members of the Urbana Worship Team ascend the left side of the stage. . . .

After leading the gathered congregation in two upbeat gospel-inflected and rock style songs, the team begins to play an energetic, jazz-inflected instrumental introduction, with two trumpets playing close harmonies over a chord riff established by the band's guitarists. The excited crowd begins clapping on the offbeats as the worship band vocalists sing in unison a prayer for the strength "to exalt and to extend Jesus' name globally." The vocalists break into three-part, gospel-inflected harmonies to express the chorus's petition: "Cover the earth with Your glory/Cover the earth with the sound of heaven." The second verse of the song continues the theme of the first: a prayer that the "sound of heaven" be used to extend God's kingdom on earth. . . . In the Urbana participants' singing of "Cover the Earth," a song that juxtaposes eschatological imagery from various biblical sources, the dominion of God's kingdom covering the earth is represented by sound. The chorus's repeated prayer ("Cover the earth with your glory!") asks for God to bring God's kingdom to earth, represented sonically by a "new sound" being released from heaven—a sound that is then extended to earth through the agency of singers serving as God's "instruments." Speech, song, and shouting—the joyful sounds of the faithful—are all sonic agents in preparing the way for God's kingdom to come to earth.[2]

Worship in the context of InterVarsity's campus fellowships was dramatically changing too. John, a student from a university in Wisconsin, was seeing more African American and Hmong students in his fellowship.[3] He, like many other student leaders, needed to expand his worship practices, evangelism and leadership to adapt to the increasing diversity. John connected with the newer students, local leaders and worship leaders within InterVarsity who had been leading in a multicultural context. In local fellowships, college students and campus ministers were also attempting to explore what glorifying God looked like in diverse settings.

In each season of the journey for InterVarsity the question asked was not, What do we prefer in worship? or even What do students prefer in worship? As a movement they had to reimagine worship for a changing student generation. Today, many of our churches and worshiping communities are wrestling with these same questions. Our denominations and parachurch organizations are feeling the same growing pains and maybe even encountering the same messiness. It is no longer a question of whether we like or want diversity. The church *is* diverse. And congregational worship should reflect the diversity of God's people, even if a local congregation itself is not diverse.

I was one of the InterVarsity student worship leaders during the seasons of change, so I know it wasn't just about being ahead of the curve. I was heavily involved leading a small group, a worship team and a gospel choir. I attended camps and conferences. I remember Urbana 96 as a volunteer staff, and I stood on the stage with fear and trembling as we led students in worship during Urbana 03. Questions about worship and culture shaped me. I have leaned into these questions as I've collaborated with worship leaders across the country for events such as Christian Community Development Association gatherings and Evangelical Immigration Table prayer summits. And I have collaborated with colleagues to imagine worship for the changing church as I've led worship and facilitated seminars for the Willow Creek Association and Calvin Symposium on Worship. These opportunities and challenges so deeply affected me that as a seminary student I took them into my classes on church history, theology, preaching and worship. We have explored this messy way forward in the Evangelical Covenant Church and the Christian Reformed

Church (CRC), with whom I've consulted and had fellowship. These burning questions drive people to my seminars on multiethnic worship and reconciliation. Sitting with these questions, creating new paradigms in community and exploring opportunities to shape people's imagination in diverse worship for almost two decades has led me to deep values and principles that I want to share with everyone.

I wish I could offer "Multicultural Worship in a Box," but it doesn't exist. I offer only stories of roads walked, painful blisters and things learned along the journey: a breadth of application based on principles and values. This book describes a range of options and contexts. I have had the honor of working with worship leaders from varied ethnic, racial and socioeconomic backgrounds. They too have walked, blistered and learned with me. I write this book to honor them and the work we have done to develop resources for the church. I'm writing now because this is the right moment.

Because this is a topic with a variety of opinions, it feels like a huge risk to write about it. But I think the time has come to explore this together. As you read, I hope you will think of your own stories and examples. None of us has the answers—it's not one-size-fits-all—but collectively we can imagine new ways.

Expressions of worship help capture the imagination of congregants. And through worship we experience the now-but-not-yet of God's kingdom: unity, freedom and justice now—but not yet. Therefore we must create worship services that enable prophetic imagination in which people can see the future reality of God's kingdom breaking into the present. Justo González says, "Christian worship is, among other things, the place where we catch a glimpse of 'the future Reign from which and toward which God calls us'—a glimpse that both supports us in our pilgrimage and judges us in our attempts to be too settled."[4]

Worship is the communal gathering of God's people in which we glorify God for his person and actions. When I use the word *worship* I will be speaking of the congregational aspect, not of the holistic definition, which includes every aspect of our lifestyle. This definition has been shaped by time spent in the Scriptures, in community, with mentors and other authors on worship. The following are two other definitions of *worship* that have influenced me.

Worship refers to the self-expression of a particular church community in a public celebration of its faith. It has both vertical and horizontal dimensions: one's relation to God and one's relationships with fellow worshipers. It is an expression of adoration and praise to God in community.[5]

To worship is to know, to feel, to experience the resurrected Christ in the midst of the gathered community. It is breaking into the Shekinah (glory) of God, or better yet, being invaded by the Shekinah (glory) of God.[6]

Multiethnic worship acknowledges and honors the diversity of people in the local and global church, and teaches congregations to understand and honor that same diversity. Through the expressions and themes of congregational worship the call to unity is taken seriously. Ron Man, director of Worship Resources International, describes diverse worship as "the mixing of historic, traditional, contemporary, and global expressions of worship into a diverse mosaic of praise with the goal of glorifying God by encouraging the united participation of believers across demographic and generational lines."[7]

I am excited to explore approaches, forms and styles of multicultural worship that will launch us into the next season of the church. My passion is to share how people have been creating spaces and places of worship which can serve as models that will inspire us to future thinking. If anyone can learn from the trial and error of my generation, this book will have been a success.

We need the Holy Spirit to empower us for the work of calling all the nations to worship God together. It takes power beyond our skills, ability and proposed models. When we consider what it takes to call people to self-emptying, risk and change in the church, we should proceed only with a healthy dose of fear and trembling. For this reason each chapter will end with a few questions for personal reflection and prayer.

My journey as a worshiper, worship leader and pastor has been centered around the table: an image that communicates friendship, commitment and intimacy. Through this image I hope to show how our worship can foster reconciliation—inviting and including each other, sharing leadership and allowing for all God's people to worship together regardless of our various backgrounds. This book is a product of my path of learning how to lead worship in a multiethnic world where culture, ethnicity and history intersect for God's people around the world and on the block.

How do we lead worship in communities that are growing increasingly diverse? How do I get my congregation onboard with multiethnic worship? Is it even necessary? It's my hope that with the Lord's Table as our guiding image, we can foster in the church a place where everyone can come to worship together.

one

TENSION AT THE TABLE

Challenges and Opportunities
in Diverse Worship

W hy are you forcing me to sing in other languages? That's not at all helpful to my personal worship. We should have worship in a way everyone can participate." These words came from a twenty-something Asian American college student. His question was sincere—he really wanted to worship God in a meaningful way. His statement was also ridiculous, but to understand why, the backstory is necessary.

DINNER BELL IN SWAZILAND

A few years back I had the honor of visiting Swaziland, Africa. In my time there I was able to connect with a couple of local women with whom I am still in contact today. As we visited sites of Christian caregivers for HIV victims, we had time for walking, talking and singing. In one of the experiences I had the opportunity to sit with some young women (ages 14-18). It was hard to communicate with Naky, Boledi, Fikile and Kayise given that they did not speak English and I did not speak Kiswati. We made lots of gestures, smiled and laughed a lot. I told them (through a translator) that I was a worship leader and would love to hear some of their worship songs. "Could they teach me one?" I asked the interpreter. "Yes, we can teach you one," she said. (She too was a worship leader.) They shared with me the meaning and melody of the song. As they taught it to me, the women in nearby homes began to sing with them—stirring soup and singing, hanging laundry and singing, caring for a neighbor and singing "*Siyabonga Jesu* (We thank you, Jesus), *Wahamba Nathi, Siyabonga* (You walked with us; Lord, we thank you)."

We spent the rest of the evening singing to and learning from one another. It was an amazing experience I will never forget. An evening of worship with four young Swazi women in a rural community, sitting together at the table singing. It was a glimpse—a foretaste of God's kingdom in Revelation 4 and 7 where those "from every nation, tribe, people and language" stand before the throne and worship God together along with the living creatures around the throne who "day and night . . . never stop saying, 'Holy, holy, holy is the Lord God Almighty,' who was, and is, and is to come." Imagine catching a glimpse of what is written in Revelation 7:9-12:

> After this I looked, and there before me was a great multitude that no one could count, from every nation, tribe, people and language, standing before the throne and before the Lamb. They were wearing white robes and were holding palm branches in their hands. And they cried out in a loud voice:
>
> "Salvation belongs to our God,
> who sits on the throne,
> and to the Lamb."
>
> All the angels were standing around the throne and around the elders and the four living creatures. They fell down on their faces before the throne and worshiped God, saying:

"Amen!
Praise and glory
and wisdom and thanks and honor
and power and strength
be to our God for ever and ever.
Amen!"

Months later, I was directing worship at Urbana 12, in which tens of thousands of college students had gathered, to invite them to consider God's heart for global mission. The worship is planned to expose students to the global church in all of its beauty. One of the evenings we celebrated the work and lives of those caregivers I had met in Swaziland. We partnered with their work by assembling the medical care kits that the workers use as a part of the worship time. It was an evening of testimonies, videos, musical worship, prayer and action. As hosts, we knew that the reality of the situation in Swaziland would make the worship participants sad, and though lament is important, I wanted to also share the strength and hope of these caregivers who often sang in worship on their long walks to serve others. What feels sad to us is simply life for them, and the last thing we wanted was for people to walk away thinking, *How sad for these poor Africans. Let's pray for them and help them because they need us.* Instead we hoped the experience would be one of mutual exchange. We were being invited by the caregivers to be partners, yet we had something to receive from them as well. Through their strength and hope we learned what it means to follow God and to live mission in the midst of struggle. We joined their lament and hope, singing: "*Siyabonga Jesu* (We thank you, Jesus), *Wahamba Nathi, Siyabonga* (You walked with us, Lord, we thank you)."

The musical worship, prayers and videos played a huge role in creating an atmosphere of celebration, power and party. We sang, we confessed, we lamented the injustice and pain, and we responded with cries and hope. During times of congregational worship I introduced the songs I had learned from my friends. I did not have the time to share all that my heart was feeling, but I could teach them that diverse worship is not about singing a cool African song I once heard. Multicultural worship is not entertainment. It is an act of solidarity with communities we may never meet. It is connecting our story to their story, through which the Holy Spirit brings communion. That night I brought thousands of students to a table outside a house in rural Swaziland to sing with my four young friends.

However, not everyone wanted to come to that table. The young student I mentioned earlier was very frustrated. During a seminar explaining diverse worship he shared his desire for "normal" worship. Even though thousands of students at the conference came from different cultures and backgrounds, his preference was English, rock, contemporary Christian music (CCM). He assumed this was the form or style *everyone* could relate to. The conclusion was also rooted in his value for individual worship, which was interesting given the fact that he was responding to our corporate worship. This is what instigated his question: "Why are you forcing me to sing in other languages? That's not at all helpful to my personal worship. We should have worship in a way everyone can participate."

When I heard this, I experienced the most odd and powerful filling of the Holy Spirit, and began to address his question. I stood up and the words echoing Revelation 4 came out of my mouth.

The picture at the end is of the nations before the throne singing and yelling "Holy, holy, holy." People from every tongue, nation, tribe and language giving glory to God in all of their splendor. Day and night they'll yell, and they won't stop, "Holy, holy, holy." The practice of worship here on earth is to reflect, point to and practice that ultimate worship experience. We come together as a community for corporate worship so that we are not solely focused on our own personal worship. If you don't want to be distracted by other forms of music or languages you don't prefer, stay at home and press play on your iPod. Sorry if it feels inauthentic to you, it will be the authentic way of the kingdom![1]

There was silence and barely a dry eye in the room. I've been preaching, speaking and facilitating for a couple decades, and I had never experienced that sensation before. It was as if through his Word in me God's Spirit was compelling these young folks to look beyond what they were comfortable with to the new and more real reality that will come! That particular man came to me afterwards and thanked me for my exhortation. *God invites us to come to his table in unity. That has always and will continue to cause tension, given the diverse nature of his people. This is particularly pronounced in worship, where people desire authentic spaces to express themselves.*

Perhaps you may have these same questions about worship. Maybe you're thinking, *Diverse worship is great for a missions conference but not for my local congregation.* Or perhaps you like multiethnic worship but don't have a framework for why the church should do it. Perhaps others have approached you with these same questions, which is why you've picked up this book. Many communities do multiethnic worship, but they don't know why they are doing it. It may be for pragmatic reasons: their congregation is changing. It may be because they want more _____ [insert a group here] in their church. Many feel the pressure to stay current with worship trends. *The primary reasons we should pursue multicultural worship, however, are neither pragmatic nor trends, but biblical community and mission.*

AWKWARD DINNER PARTY

Sandrita, venga a comer! Growing up, I heard my mom shout out the window for us to "come and eat" more times than I can remember. This call told us that the time had come for us to gather as a family. We'd not only eat a great meal of *arroz con pollo* (a Colombian rice-and-chicken dish) but we'd also be forced to share about the best and worst part of our day, our highs and our lows. This was our family tradition.

Christians also have a table at the center of our family tradition. Many scriptural images talk about table fellowship. In the Old Testament, sharing a meal with someone was a sign of friendship and esteem. An invitation to a banquet table was a huge honor and showed that the person was valued and trusted by the host. In the New Testament, Jesus spent much time eating and teaching at tables (Matthew 26:7; Luke 5:29-32; 7:36-50; 14:1-24). Jesus was also breaking rules that had been added to the table by sharing the space with women and tax collectors.[2] Even in Jesus' last days the table was the place of his final instructions, including a command to continue to gather at the table in remembrance of him (1 Corinthians 11:23-26). Meals were full of significance and order, and provided a way for God's people to experience him as they connected with one another.

> A meal was never simply a time to ingest food and quench thirst; at meals people displayed kinship and friendship. Meals themselves—the foods served, the manner in which that was done and by whom—carried socially significant, coded communication. The messages had to do with honor, social rank in the family and community, belonging and purity, or holiness. Social status and role were acted out in differentiated tasks and expectations around meals, and the maintenance of balance and harmony at meals was crucial to

the sense of overall well-being. Among God's chosen people, meals became ways of experiencing and enjoying God's presence and provision.[3]

Likewise in worship, as we connect with each other in community, we encounter God. If the worship experience and practice is filled with people coming from different ethnic backgrounds, social ranks and ways of eating, then there will be opportunity to enjoy God's presence together. This guiding image of communion at the Table of Christ is central to why we participate in cross-cultural worship. The table communicates fellowship with others (across differences, as Jesus modeled) and with God.

One of my favorite places to encounter Christ at table is in Luke 14, which illustrates a master's invitation to a great banquet feast. The master's invitation list reveals no favoritism at the table. All are invited the banquet: the social elite as well as those from the highways and byways. The tension mounts: people from different ethnic and socioeconomic standings gather. The result: awkward dinner conversations. And let's face it, we tend to avoid parties where we expect awkwardness.

But isn't being at the Lord's Table in the church like being at an awkward party? Imagine a dinner where random strangers from all walks of life—poor, rich, old, young—are invited. There they are, staring at one another across the table wondering what they can possibly say and why the other is dressed like *that*. This is the church! The church consists of people from *every* walk of life, profession, culture, nationality, race and background. We come together at God's invitation. The table is an intimate and unique place of communion; shouldn't we Christians be able to share a meal without the painful moments of disconnect? It would be easy if we were all clones, but God in his wisdom did not create us that way. As individuals we are different, and as communities we are different. The way we communicate and relate is shaped by culture, and the result is tension and awkwardness.

The awkwardness we experience when sharing a table cross-culturally can be present for many reasons.

1. *Lack of exposure.* When I was visiting friends in Cairo, they served me a dish of slimy green soup. I stared down at it and the tension began to show on my face. It was molokhia, which is similar to kale but with three times the calcium. It was delicious!

2. *Preference.* In Northern China many of the families we visited served us mutton dishes. Lamb is not my favorite.

3. *Fear.* Given that my mother is from Colombia, I decided to sponsor a World Vision child from a slum outside of her hometown. When my sister and I went to visit, our hosts served us a water-based mango drink. We consumed it and prayed for our digestive system.

On a recent trip to Portugal my Portuguese friend Pedro publicly made fun of me for eating with my fork in my right hand. He told me that he can tell who in a restaurant is American because they put their knife on the plate and move their fork from their left to their right hand. He said putting your knife on the plate lacked etiquette in most European countries. I immediately jumped online and looked it up in order to defend myself. Sure enough, there are different styles of cutting and eating food, and I was being offensive in this context. I imagine that there are dozens, if not hundreds, of cultural cues we give off when sharing a meal. The food at the table, the way we cut our food, and whether we use utensils at all give away our country of origin, cultural background and maybe even socioeconomic status. Pedro and I went back and forth for a bit, but in the end we decided that language wasn't the only thing that we didn't share in common. We ate, laughed and thought about the many difficult and awkward moments there are to share crossculturally. When people come to the table across differences, tension is not necessarily because people dislike one another. Tension exists because we each carry a particular set of norms that we subconsciously live into.

CHALLENGE

One of the greatest challenges of our generation is that people make choices based almost exclusively on preferences. We have hundreds of restaurant choices, and if we want to stay home we order online or call. The options are endless. And we view our Christian practices (church, podcast, worship) similarly. We navigate all the choices by means of personal preference. Picture someone who doesn't like a certain TV show. If asked why, she might say it's just not her thing. Insisting on multiethnic worship runs against the grain of that kind of personal preference. People might think African American worship or songs in Mandarin or Spanish are okay for some, but diverse worship just is not their thing. They may not understand that worship in community is more about *us* than about *me*. Conversations about worship are often contentious due to the energy behind people's preferences. Like many of our faith practices (preaching, Scripture study, prayer and leadership), both biblical principles and cultural preferences are at play.

Intentional multiethnic worship provides great challenges. It reflects our culture of preferences; there is a lot of variety, and individuals have many choices depending on the service they choose (or even within services). But it can also be countercultural because sometimes one specific dish is served. Imagine a group of friends deciding what to do for lunch. In the past, places with limited menus were the only option. Then, as Americans became more open to other foods, menus became more diverse. Today, we can eat in community without having to share the same type of food.

Sometimes, though, like at the Wednesday night small group at my home, only one dish is served. My husband and I always cook for our small group, which spends one hour around the table doing life, and one hour studying Scripture and praying. This ethnically diverse community eats whatever we serve them. Sometimes they have to ask what they are eating, because they are having Indian for the first time, but they still try it. We have not yet had a group member stop attending because of the variety of food or the fact that their preferences are not being met.[4] We do have people with gluten and dairy allergies, so we are intentional about the food. But all are gracious guests who are open to our sriracha mayo chicken and kimchi rice, or chipotle rub chuletas (pork chops) or whatever happens to be on sale that week at the store.[5]

OPPORTUNITY

The world is increasingly diverse, and the church has the opportunity to welcome worshipers. If we do not develop worship practices that resonate with a variety of people's longings, we may lose more people. What are some opportunities we might have to welcome new people into our faith communities? Who is missing? Where is their potential for growth and inclusion? The three categories of people we should keep our eye on are unchurched, millennials and people of color.

Unchurched. Let's consider the unchurched. The number of religiously unaffiliated people in our society is on the rise. Some have called this "the rise of the nones."[6] This is particularly pronounced among adults under thirty, a third of whom are unaffiliated.[7] Yet, even though they are unaffiliated, two-thirds of them claim to be spiritual or to believe in God.[8] They are not hostile to Christianity but not connected to a church. Certainly, most of us have acquaintances—whether on campus, in the workplace or the neighborhood—in this group. They generally believe faith-based communities are good for society but find them suspect because they do not reflect their cultural realities. They think religious organizations are too focused on money, power, politics and rules, so looking for a church does not interest them.

Millennials. Age matters! Generational shifts in the church are being captured by organizations such as the Barna Millennials Project, dedicated to research in the area of the next generation of Christians.[9] The Barna research echoes the research from the Public Religion Research Institute, which notes that white Christians make up only 25 percent of younger Americans, but nearly 70 percent of older Americans are white Christians. "That's a remarkable demographic change."[10] For the majority church there is a huge opportunity to engage our young people if we make our worship spaces relevant to their everyday.

People of color. The face of Christianity is diversifying. In addition to the unchurched and millennials, the church is becoming more diverse. This may be why so much church planting is happening in diverse communities. While the white community is becoming less religious, people of color are not. You can see that by looking at the aggregated data from surveys conducted by the Pew Research Center, which states that one-fifth of all white Americans consider themselves unaffiliated—up 5 percent from 2007—but the numbers of unaffiliated blacks and Hispanics have not risen.[11] According to the Public Religion Research Institute, over half of young American Christians (ages 18 to 29) are people of color.[12] What an incredible opportunity we have to reshape worship for the increasingly diverse church. I've consulted with older white congregations in urban settings who have a desire to worship in ways that captivate their Asian immigrant refugees. I've also worked with African American congregations who are seeking to respond to the wave of first-generation Central Americans in their neighborhood. The world is moving from everywhere to everywhere, which is seen daily in print articles and TV coverage of current events.

The US church has spent decades fighting worship wars, which focus on things that may be less relevant given the current challenges and opportunities. When we talk about the need for our young people to connect to tradition and legacy (which I believe is critical), we need to examine our assumptions about demographics and the values of young people and their connectedness to the church. The church is and always has been a global faith, but in the past much of the worship-wars conversation has been dominated by Western voices and leadership. But in this new generation a majority of our future leaders will be nonwhite and non-Western. Maybe it's time to broaden the conversation.

While consumerism and individual preferences in worship is a problem, we must imagine a new church reflective of the people who will be present, and allow that image to shape our conversations. Our unprecedented access to the cultures and circumstances of communities around the world has given us the ability to better connect to the global church. The same amount of energy and focused critique that has been given to the worship wars needs to be transferred to our need to connect across cultures. Let's look back to history, out at the world and forward to the future.

WORSHIP AND CULTURE

At the table where all God's people worship together, we must recognize that worship is both contextual and crosscultural. When the Calvin Institute of Christian Worship articulated their ten core convictions about worship, they identified having "an open and discerning approach to culture" as one of their convictions.[13] They stated,

> Worship should strike a healthy balance among four approaches or dimensions to its cultural context: worship is

transcultural (some elements of worship are beyond culture), contextual (worship reflects the culture in which it is offered), cross-cultural (worship breaks barriers of culture through worship), and counter-cultural (worship resists the idolatries of its cultural context.[14]

For a worship culture to be developed with integrity to the local expression, it is imperative to do the work of contextualization, which considers the context, place or location. It is important to explore the local elements of liturgy: language, posture, gesture, hymnody, music, art and so on. This will allow us to avoid mistakes made in the past, which imposed forms of worship foreign to a culture.

As people of faith in a multiethnic world, we must all practice the discipline of anthropology, which studies the development of human culture at the level of beliefs and behavior. This implies that the culture and context are meaningful to the local expression of worship in the church. Jesus is the Savior of all people; *every* culture has gifts, and he welcomes their treasure as ways to honor and glorify him. All the nations of the earth will display their cultural gifts in worship to the King of glory.

> I saw no temple in the city, for the Lord God Almighty and the Lamb are its temple. And the city has no need of sun or moon, for the glory of God illuminates the city, and the Lamb is its light. The nations will walk in its light, and the kings of the world will enter the city in all their glory.... And all the nations will bring their glory and honor into the city. (Revelation 21:22-24, 26, NLT)

In the end the beloved community, which consists of people from every nation, tribe, people and language, worships God. This breathtaking family will be present in all of its beauty. The kings and the nations will bring their glorious gifts into the city of God.

There will be sounds, smells, movement and colors that point to the creative nature of God and his people. There won't be a corner of heaven for the quiet worshipers and another for the dancers. Since we on this side of history have seen the season finale, our call is to live as a foretaste of that reality. We are to celebrate and desire all the God-given gifts that communities bring in worship. Revelation reminds us that when all is restored and God's shalom reigns, the gifts of the nations will be visible and present.

Are the gifts of the nations visible to you? Do you have a sense that the world is bigger and God is greater because of your encounters with people in other cultures? People who travel, or love to explore new cultures locally, know that there is great beauty to be discovered. The sights and flavors of different communities sometimes go beyond interesting to fantastic. The gifts of the nations are visible to us in the architecture and art of other cultures: the magnificent pyramids of Egypt, the Roman aqueducts, the Moorish-influenced structures of southern Spain, and the incredible skyscrapers of Chicago. The ability of people to create and flourish in such distinct ways reminds us that we are made in the image of our Creator. He did not make mere flowers or fish, but so many different species of each that we have entire sciences dedicated to detailing their distinctiveness. Humankind is given the responsibility to take care of creation, to be fruitful and to multiply. Humanity, made in God's likeness, bears God's image. The fact that we bear the *imago Dei* (image of God) means we too participate in creation. Scholars call this the cultural mandate, and it is rooted in God's command in Genesis.

> Then God said, "Let us make mankind in our image, in our likeness, so that they may rule over the fish in the sea and the birds in the sky, over the livestock and all the wild animals, and over all the creatures that move along the ground."

So God created mankind in his own image,
> in the image of God he created them;
> male and female he created them.

God blessed them and said to them, "Be fruitful and increase in number; fill the earth and subdue it. Rule over the fish in the sea and the birds in the sky and over every living creature that moves on the ground." (Genesis 1:26-28)

Though we all have gifts to offer, all humanity has been affected by sin. This is made evident in Genesis 3, where sin is introduced into creation. From that point forward, everything is both beautiful and broken at the same time. Therefore every global culture must be valued, explored *and* critiqued. All aspects of culture are stained by the mess of sin, but all cultures have the mark of creative beauty. In *Culture Making* Andy Crouch says,

> The gospel, even though it is deeply embedded in Jewish cultural history, is available in the "mother tongue" of every human being. There is no culture beyond its reach—because the very specific cultural story of Israel was never anything other than a rescue mission for all the cultures of the world, initiated by the world's Creator.
>
> This sudden explosion of cultural diversity within the people of God does not mean that all cultures, and all cultural artifacts and traditions, are simply baptized and declared good. Instead, what Acts sets off is a vast and lengthy process of cultural discernment, of which the letter from the Jewish Christians in Jerusalem to their Gentile counterparts in Antioch was just the beginning.[15]

The practice of worship is no different. The exploration of music, worship and culture is the discipline of ethnodoxology. It studies the ways people worship God in diverse cultures.

Dr. Robin Harris, president of the International Council of Ethnodoxologists, states,

> In the late 1990s worship leader and missionary Dave Hall coined the term "ethnodoxology" by combining three Greek terms—*ethne* (peoples), *doxa* (glory), and *logos* (word). The English word *doxology* combines "words" and "glory" into a concept signifying "words to glorify" or "worship" God.[16]

Becoming students of culture as it pertains to worship helps us to grow and adapt with the changing demographic of the church, and live into the vision of Revelation 21. When we come to the table we must look around, see how people are seated, what the interaction is like and how they are using their utensils (if there are any at all), and we may need to ask what we are eating. It's easy to recognize others' cuisine as uniquely ethnic. We even have food aisles in the grocery store for ethnic food. But are only certain foods rooted in a cultural context? No, it merely means the grocery store owner sees the other twenty aisles as normal food. But Mexican, Asian and maybe even Italian food is "ethnic" or "other." In reality we are all ethnic; Mexicans have Mexican food every night. It's just food. They don't say, "Let's have Mexican tonight!" They just cook.

Worship is not only contextual but also crosscultural; it has the potential to connect the narratives of people. Revelation 7:9-12, with its depiction of a multitude "from every nation, tribe, people and language, standing before the throne and before the Lamb," gives us a picture of the kingdom community at the end of time. This passage, while familiar, should never become boring. Clearly, it's a supernatural vision. The authority of the Lamb, Christ himself, the power of the Spirit and the majesty of God are the only things that can unite a group of people from all over the world in a common anthem! Pay attention to one day's news: civil unrest, war,

ethnic cleansing, genocide, abuse and racism plague our relationships crossculturally. I wish this was true only outside the church,
but our history demands that we take a good look in the mirror
and cry out to the only God who is worthy,

> Salvation belongs to our God,
> who sits on the throne,
> and to the Lamb. . . .

> Amen!
> Praise and glory
> and wisdom and thanks and honor
> and power and strength
> be to our God for ever and ever.
> Amen!

This vision of the end can only be hoped for and lived into by recognizing how far we are from it, and the beauty and awe we will
experience when we participate in it.

Our faith calls us not only to dream and hope for this day, but
also Scripture calls us to be a foretaste of the kingdom now. We
today should live in the reality of the kingdom and witness what is
to come. The church points to the time that is coming by modeling
and living into it today. We ought not be influenced by what we
see around us; we should instead live into a worship that models
something distinct from the rest of the world.

> Therefore, I urge you, brothers and sisters, in view of God's
> mercy, to offer your bodies as a living sacrifice, holy and
> pleasing to God—this is your true and proper worship. Do
> not conform to the pattern of this world, but be transformed
> by the renewing of your mind. . . .

> Love must be sincere. Hate what is evil; cling to what is
> good. Be devoted to one another in love. Honor one another

above yourselves. Never be lacking in zeal, but keep your spiritual fervor, serving the Lord. Be joyful in hope, patient in affliction, faithful in prayer. Share with the Lord's people who are in need. Practice hospitality. (Romans 12:1-2, 9-13)

Biblical community is lived out across many differences: racial, cultural, ethnic, socioeconomic, theological. In the practice of corporate worship, no matter how different we are, we share in one common narrative in which we remember we are collectively the people of God. Yes, we are many nations. Yes, those differences are significant and beautiful. Yes, they cause natural tensions. In worship, however, we recite, reflect and remember that God has joined us together to learn from one another how to best glorify him as a corporate body.

The church has always been and will always be a multiethnic, multilingual, global community. How then do we capture people's imagination in an embodied experience in worship? How do we create space for the vision of God's people to be realized? Does everyone have to be at the same table every time? How can I learn to lead others toward this goal? These are the questions we will explore in the coming chapters.

KEY CONCEPTS

- Worship is cultural and contextual.
- God calls us to worship him together across cultures.
- Cultural preferences and differences inevitably lead to tension.
- God intended diversity, and we should live into the future reality of the kingdom now.

FOR REFLECTION

- What are some of the tensions in your worship context?

- How would you describe your congregation's worship style (e.g., reflective, exuberant, liturgical, unplanned)?

- Ask your worship team, pastor and congregants how they would describe your congregation's worship style. Do they agree?

- Visit a church of a different background than yours. Watch and learn. What is similar? What is different?

FOR DISCUSSION

- Is your fellowship, congregation or ministry embarking on a journey of multiethnic worship? What are two next steps toward leading your congregation on this path?

- Some people may be resistant to growing in the area of worship. If so, what are the obstacles in their way, and how can these obstacles be addressed?

- How has your context changed over the last ten years in regard to the unchurched, youth and diversity? How has your worship changed as a result?

Prayer: We praise you, Lord, for making your creation so incredibly beautiful; help me to see the beauty in the diversity of your creation.

- two -

IS PB&J ETHNIC FOOD?

The Myth of Normal Worship

Peanut butter and jelly is a delicious American creation. Having grown up in America, I've regularly enjoyed it. It's also extremely efficient. Don't have time to make lunch? PB&J. Out of groceries? PB&J. Need some quick protein while writing a book on multiethnic worship? PB&J. It's normal for us to find peanut butter in our kitchen. But to what extent can we say it's normal? Consider the following story:

Every year [a] state sends an educational tester to [Holly's] classroom. The first year, almost all the kids in Holly's class failed the basic academic test for kindergarten. They could not follow sequences. Their vocabulary was inadequate. The report came back concluding that the kids all needed special ed.

Holly's observation was, "This is a fairly average class. Maybe one or two could use some special tutoring, but most of the kids are normal. Some are very smart." So she asked the tester to return. As the test was repeated, Holly learned that to measure sequencing the white evaluator had asked each kid to explain the stages of making a peanut butter and jelly sandwich. This should be fairly simple for a five-year-old, but they all failed. Why? What was happening?

Holly realized, *None of these kids eat PBJ; they eat burritos and tamales for lunch. They're all Latino.* "Why don't you ask them what are the stages of making a burrito?" she suggested. All the kids but one passed this test. They passed easily, explaining clearly and sequentially how to make a burrito. That year they stayed out of special ed.[1]

PB&J may be the most delicious cultural food that exists, but the fact is that the test assumed all American children would know how to describe its creation because it's so normal. When the church invites others to the table in worship, what assumptions do we make about what is and is not normal?

NORMAL WORSHIP

Normal is something that occurs naturally: a pattern for how things should be. Describing something as normal implies it is regular and natural not only for us but for the people around us as well. We use the word *normal* to describe not only what is but what should be natural for everyone. We are comforted by normal. We assimilate to normal. There is a lot of power in naming something as normative. In the case of the PB&J kids, the assumption that they naturally should be able to describe how a PB&J sandwich is made limited how their intelligence was evaluated. Basically, PB&J is "normal," but arepas and spicy rice cakes are "ethnic." This similarly happens in the church For instance, a US church denomination recently said that nearly a quarter of its congregations identified themselves as being ethnic. Does this mean the rest are ethnicity free? By positioning ethnic minority cultures against white cultures we're defining what is normal. In reality all congregations are ethnic.

Over decades of hosting conversations about worship, I have seen this principle applied in conscious and subconscious ways. *We* are normal, but everyone else has a hyphenated culture. We are normal, but everyone not like us is *other*. We do not realize that the way we do things is locked in a set of values and beliefs deeply influenced by cultural factors (denominational, generational, gender, ethnic, racial and socioeconomic). The biggest barrier Christians face in developing communities hospitable to people of every ethnicity and culture is their ignorance about their own culture. We are unaware of what it means to be *us* and hyper aware of what it means to be *them*. This is interesting given that many leadership and spiritual-formation concepts used in the church revolve around self-awareness. We assess our spiritual gifts, temperament, strengths, conflict styles, leadership preferences and emotional intelligence in order to gain more clarity on our impact as individuals. While we desire to grow in effectiveness and invest significantly in individual self-awareness, we do not consider organizational culture.

The hardest part of the journey for many of us starts with self-awareness. A few years back at the Willow Creek Arts Conference, I was asked to lead a seminar on worship and culture. The supplied title was "The Curse of the White Suburban Worship Leader."

Surprise! The curse was the fact that those who attended didn't know they had a culture. This eye-opening information invited them on a journey of understanding that their PB&J-eating culture was indeed ethnic. The energy was fantastic as people described their worship services to one another in contrast to the cultural expressions they had experienced in urban churches they had visited or worship they had experienced overseas. It made them move from describing their worship as boring or normal to more concrete values and descriptions. At the end of our time together they were more aware of their own culture. The reality is that we all need this revelation moment.

This is not an issue for white people alone. Esther, a young Korean American woman, had been a congregant at a Mexican church in Los Angeles for over a decade. While discussing culture with church leaders she suggested that to welcome people from different cultures the Mexican culture of the church would likely need to change. "Well, I don't see us as a Mexican church," one of the leaders stated. The others in the room echoed this statement. Despite 90 percent of the congregants being Mexican, including all but one of the staff members, they couldn't see how Mexican they were. Esther had been a part of white, black and Asian American fellowships, so she was able to clearly identify what her brothers and sisters saw as normal was actually distinct.

As a way of training pastors, musicians and worship teams, I often take them on church visits. This is a fun experience because I get to see how God is at work in a variety of expressions of the church, and I get to be present when the power of cultural preference becomes real for people. People usually do two things on such visits. First, they point out all of the commonalities between the service and their "normal" experience. Second, they compliment the commonalities. A typical statement is, "I liked how they used a full band just like we do at my church." On one visit I took Susan, a Chinese American woman, to an urban church that was primarily African American. She clearly enjoyed the worship. I asked her what she thought of the service, and she replied with positive statements, including,

- "Three of the songs they sang were just like us."
- "They used a band and sound system just like us."
- "There were families of all ages just like us."

When I asked her what differences she saw, she said she felt there were more commonalities. Good Christian answer! I then asked her if she would choose to meet regularly with this community. "No," she responded, expressing herself quite forcefully. She continued, "It's just *so* different. The service was so long, and the sound system way too loud for me. And even though we sang the same songs, they each lasted thirteen minutes. I felt very out of place." Her discomfort and preferences came out only after I asked her if she could see herself making that her "normal" church.

Jamaya, an African American leader, described her first awareness of worship culture when she participated in a primarily white worship event. "The person leading the worship service urged us all to respond in prayer. I got up from my chair, ran to the front and started shouting my prayers to the Lord. After all, this is what we did in my COGIC church at home.[2] I realized I was the only one who responded that way." This was normal prayer time for her. As she spent time with the community, she realized her prayer was not normal for all, but it was for COGIC. She learned to adapt, allowing herself to be formed by her new community. In time she also introduced her friends to her "normal." Her expressiveness is not a sign of superior faith; neither was the more reserved form of prayer. Each has conformed to different patterns of emotional expression.

One Sunday I asked Karl, my husband, how church was. He recounted all of the powerful ways God had met them in prayer and worship. Then he added, "Well, I got there late. At 10:06 the person leading prayer said, 'We're still in prayer even though service time already started.' Then, the song from the prayer service lasted eleven more minutes. So, who knows how long they had been repeating it." Karl's cultural values made him alert to the exact timing of worship and how long things lasted. He enjoys worship at our church. He has worshiped in churches with various expressions. The fact that he noted time does not mean he is less spiritual. The fact that this congregation was not concerned with time does not make them more spiritual. They are conforming to different natural patterns around time and event orientation.

Identifying cultural norms is not just an individual activity. It is also important for communities. When I serve with crosscultural teams or in crosscultural environments, I utilize a resource called the cultural continuum, which helps groups identify values in the areas of time, communication, expressiveness, relationship and space. When you complete this chapter, spend some time with your community reflecting on your own culture and that of your community. What do you define as "normal"?

GOOD WORSHIP

We believe that good worship will draw people, but what is "good" or "excellent" worship? I was sharing a vision for inclusive worship with a multicultural community of college students. While the group was ethnically diverse, the leadership was not. That meant that the way we did things did not embrace all the ethnic groups represented in our community. People would visit and celebrate how many students of color were present in contrast to most of the other student fellowships, which were primarily white. The community felt proud that people of different hues were present in the room, but that was not enough for me. What good was it to have a diverse community represented if the culture did not reflect the beauty of those communities? More than that, what about the other ethnic groups on campus who were not being intentionally reached? What if our community could develop spaces of hospitality where people of different ethnic backgrounds felt not only represented but also welcomed? I shared the vision and asked for responses.

One of our leaders replied with energy and confidence, "Why do we have to try so hard to be something we are not. Why can't we just worship . . . you know *normal* worship? Why do we have to sing in Spanish? If we just have *good* worship, people from different backgrounds will come."

"What do you mean by *normal*?" I asked.

"You know, normal worship, regular worship," he said and went on to describe contemporary Christian singers and movements that were all white.

This is not just a white issue. I have heard these, or similar, words from churches of various ethnic backgrounds and generations. I have had conversations with African American worship leaders that were almost identical. These are well-intended but naive words that invite deeper dialogue. We all desperately need someone to hold up a mirror so we can see ourselves. That is the beauty of diverse community: when we encounter those who are different from us, we have the opportunity to engage in conversation in order to understand them as well as ourselves. Since early on most of my experiences had been with Asian American and white upper-middle-class young adults, I figured this attitude had to do with privilege and power. Those who were on top of society in education, economics and so forth viewed themselves as the center and therefore as normal. I quickly learned I was mistaken. Urban African American and Latino community leaders echoed the same words as I had heard before.

Recently, in a Latino worship-team meeting I had the opportunity to observe the same conversation. The church was foreseeing changes as their community demographics were changing. Early in the process a group of worship-team members and leaders gathered to envision a new worship ministry. People shared their preferences and perspectives. One person shared her criticism of the models of multiethnic worship she had seen at conferences (including mine), because it was "too intentional" and felt like people had to try too hard to lead. As the conversation escalated one person shouted out, "If our worship is *good*, people will come!

Style doesn't matter. They'd see we are worshipers and want to be at our church." Another woman (not from that dominant cultural group) disagreed by explaining that her friends would find the worship experiences too emotional. That was an interesting insight given that it was a regular practice for the worship leaders to weep and focus on expression of feelings. Many of the people (again all from the same ethnic and socioeconomic group) agreed that if the church merely focused on being good and authentic, anyone should be able to relate to the music.

Over and over I heard the same thing: "Culture does not matter. Form and style do not matter. A heart of worship is what matters. If our worship is sincere and *good*, people will come." While that is a comforting thought, demographics don't support that as reality. The form and environment do matter to how people worship. I know that to some churches good worship means lots of movement. To others it means no distractions and places for reflection. Still others believe the "anointing is obvious when you change plans," supported with comments such as "I don't know what the Lord is doing, but it's gonna be good." Another group might say good worship is prayerfully and intentionally planned by someone (often called a liturgist). Cultural preferences do matter. Our deeply held values and beliefs about what is good and right are influenced by our socioeconomic experiences.

AUTHENTIC

Humans are prone to do things that are comfortable. We either like things that come easy or that feel authentic to who we are and organic to our community. Learning to speak a language, playing new rhythms and praying in new ways are not at the top of our list of things to get excited about. I am sure you have heard people say that participating in diverse worship feels inauthentic to them. It's not natural to who they are, they don't want to dance or clap, or they don't want to sit still or cry the entire service. In cultures that value individualism we are more likely to hear that we should feel free to sit, stand or worship as we like. Often, authenticity in worship is more desirable than being formed in worship. This attitude won't work if we are trying to create spaces where we intentionally introduce crosscultural worship.

Let's face it, my Mandarin stinks! I'd rather sing in Spanish. I'd prefer to pray in English. I really like to move during worship, which would likely be a distraction in many of the churches or college chapels I visit. Crosscultural worship is just what it sounds like: we are crossing over (a bridge) to another way of doing things, which creatures of habit rarely like to do. As Spencer Perkins, the late reconciliation leader and coauthor of *More Than Equals*, used to say, "Bridge building hurts!"[3] Not only are we crossing a bridge, we are also acting as a bridge for other people to cross, which means we are always getting stepped on. It takes commitment and intentionality; it's a decision to act.

Authentic is not synonymous with *unintentional*. Intentionality is important to developing practices that become organic. In fact, spiritual formation is all about practicing disciplines that shape us. Now I've used two dirty words: *practice* and *discipline*, which I should define.

> prac·tice /praktəs/ perform an activity or exercise repeatedly or regularly in order to improve or maintain one's proficiency.

> dis·ci·pline /disəplin/ training that corrects, molds, or perfects moral character[4]

The first definition tells us that practices are not a one-time thing but a repeated pattern over a period of time. And discipline takes "training" or practice. To some of us, these are dirty words because they demand a level of commitment we are not used to. If taking a daily vitamin is hard for me, how hard do you think it is to create places of worship that form us? If we want organic produce, we pay a premium because so much intentionality goes into finding non-GMO seeds, fertilizing the soil with compost and keeping weeds and bugs away without pesticides. Just as *organic* and *intentional* are not opposites, *intentional* and *authentic* are not at odds.

Worship is not merely about authentic personal expression but also communal formation. In 2 Corinthians 3:18, we find that worship in community, by the Spirit, forms us in Christ. Paul says that "we all, with unveiled face, beholding the glory of the Lord, are being transformed into the same image from one degree of glory to another. For this comes from the Lord who is the Spirit" (esv). As we gather in community and see God's glory, the Spirit forms us. Corporate worship is key to spiritual formation and transformation because it keeps us focused on the glory of Christ. Practicing worship gives us a space where we can agree in song, prayer and Scripture. When Christ is exalted, proclaimed and experienced in our worship as truly glorious, we are changed. Congregational worship is critical. It is not merely about singing songs; it's theology to music, sermon to song. As we gather together, we come as we are, but we should leave different from how we came. The following are a few things I learned from John Witvliet, director of the Calvin Institute of Christian Worship, while collaborating on a worship course:

- Worship should be expressive and formative. The aim of corporate worship is not individual expression but communal formation of faith.

- We should practice authenticity and desire transformative worship experiences. Worship should stretch us to rehearse truths while our feelings catch up with us.

- The Psalms, which are a model for individual and corporate worship, invite us to identify or align with the experience of the psalmist regardless of our feelings.

Witvliet states,

> From the perspective of the worshiper, we need a "conversion of the imagination" to see that public worship is good not only if it "connects" with us, is "relevant" to us, but also to the extent that it helps us practice habits which strengthen our capacity for a profound, honest relationship with God and each other. We need to value how our participation is, in part, an act of alignment, learning to align our hearts, minds, and experience with words that are chosen on our behalf.[5]

Whether we come from a diverse or monocultural context, there are two primary reasons why we should engage in other cultural forms of worship. First, we experience a fuller picture of God. Not only is the variety and range of God's creativity seen and expressed in the vast artistic range of human approaches to worship (music, instruments, words, songs), but a variety of themes are also represented. Some churches would rather sing, shout and dance about God's victory to remind us that because he is powerful we can make it through another week! Others see worship as a space where we can cry out to God in our angst because he allows us to come as we are: weak and broken. Sharing these moments with one another broadens our perspective of God; he is my Rock and Deliverer and my Comforter and Healer. The second reason is that diverse worship leads to personal transformation. Our understanding of the church is transformed. As we worship crossculturally, we better understand our own worship as one piece of a larger community. It's like discovering we have an accent when we are around people from other parts of the country. As we experience our differences, we can more fully enjoy what it means to connect to the global church. Then we realize we are a part of a bigger family. This helps connect us to the hearts of our brothers and sisters whose lives are radically different from ours.[6]

THE NEXT WORSHIP

Our instinct to focus on *normal*, *good* and *authentic* keeps us from landing at the ultimate issue of *what's next*. What is the future of worship in our changing church? What spaces and places of worship does this global millennial generation of leaders need to create? The demographics in our North American context must move us to ask the question, What's next?[7] Whether your church is multiethnic or homogeneous, the influence of a globalizing world can be seen. We can spend an hour in downtown Madison, Wisconsin, or Austin, Texas, and be overwhelmed by the amount of "ethnic" food options. When our grandparents and parents were young, Italian was ethnic; now we have sixty different cultures to choose from on a Friday night.

Is the goal of real worship, then, that everyone is at the same table together? What should I do if I'm at a Christian college that is overwhelmingly monocultural? What if my church is predominantly black or brown? Great questions! (We will explore these in the next chapters.) Some leaders within multiethnic church-plant movements seem to believe that the goal is to gather all in the same room. They believe the ultimate reflection of diversity is a church with all cultures at one table. If this is true, then pragmatically most of what we do in worship would be aimed at meeting that goal. As someone who has spent almost two decades leading in the multiethnic movement both on campus and in the church, I'd love to see more than the current 13.7 percent of US congregations be multiethnic, but the reality is this is not the case.[8] The 1998 National Congregations Study identified 7.5 percent of all congregations as multiracial, and a similar study in the late 1990s reported that 5 percent of Protestant churches were multiracial.[9] Today, depending on the study, 13.7 percent to 20 percent[10] of Americans congregate in churches that could be considered multiethnic, which Michael Emerson defines as a congregation in which no one racial group makes up 80 percent or more of the people.[11]

The ultimate goal of diverse worship is not to have everyone at the same table. As we think about what's next, it is helpful to steer clear of claiming one ultimate goal, as if there is only one. The image of the body in 1 Corinthians 12 pictures many parts of the body within the local church as well as in the broader church. Therefore, different churches will have different approaches to congregational worship, but we're all part of the same body and work together to do things that we can't do on our own. One church may utilize a blend of musical styles well. A less multiethnic church may intentionally partner with the global church, while a more diverse urban church may focus on its particular community. To prescribe one type of inclusive worship is to deny each community's gifts and context. Worshiping communities will live into hospitality, solidarity and mutuality in distinct ways, both within each congregation as well as in partnership with other congregations. In "Multicultural Congregations and Worship: A Literature Review," Terry York says, "No congregation is expected to wrap its arms around the entire world. But every congregation is expected to open its arms to the entire world."[12]

To expect every church to be multiethnic would require regional churches, since our neighborhoods are frankly not always diverse. In some denominations and urban locations, the parish model makes the most sense. This model, where churches are connected to their local communities and involved in witness and presence in their neighborhoods, would mirror the diversity of their neighborhood. In the case of my current church, the neighborhood is mostly black and brown (whites typically have relocated). For us a multiethnic expression means it will be African American, Mexican and Puerto Rican. In our urban vicinity many multiethnic churches (primarily white and Asian American) are made of relocators who have moved back into the city, riding the recent wave of gentrification. They are typically socioeconomically homogeneous and do not reflect the surrounding community demographic. Global and local partnerships across churches allow us to create spaces to engage in ethnically diverse worship. Sadly, this is seldom done.

However, imagine how powerful a partnership like that could be. Say a white pastor plants a mostly white and Asian American church in a predominantly Latino neighborhood. Being new to the community the white pastor reaches out to the pastor of a Latino church with a longtime presence in the community. As a relationship grows they decide to partner in worship. At first the multiethnic church worship team visits the Latino church, celebrating God at their table. A few weeks later the multiethnic church becomes the host for the Latino worship team. Next, the worship team from each church can lead worship at the other, allowing the worship team and congregation from one fellowship to sample the "food" of the other in their own "home." A third step will be to combine teams to lead worship together at each church. What an incredible opportunity for the mostly white and Asian church to worship with their Latino brothers and sisters in the midst of challenging immigration concerns, and for the Latino church to worship with these new residents as their brothers and sisters as the neighborhood starts to change. What kind of solidarity could be created as the neighborhood's constituents, new and old, shape the future of their community?

In worship we can connect our congregations with the global church in our community and abroad, regardless of the ethnic makeup of our own community. Imagine if through worship our churches confirmed that the banquet table of the kingdom is for all. *This next worship is an inclusive and diverse table that embodies reconciliation and points to the future celebration of God's people from every tribe, tongue, people and language.*

KEY CONCEPTS

- We are all ethnic, there is no "normal"; a journey of self-awareness is critical.

- *Good* doesn't mean the same thing in all cultures.

- Our desire for authentic worship should not deter us from intentionally pursuing formation in worship.

FOR REFLECTION

- What experiences has God allowed in your life to test your understanding of normal and increase your self-awareness?

- What aspects of your worship culture do you enjoy? What aspects do you think are preferences? What aspects do you think are mandatory for all congregational worship settings?

- In your experience crossing cultures in worship, what's been difficult? Why?

FOR DISCUSSION

- How do people on your worship team define *normal*, *good* and *authentic* worship?

- Spend time with your community evaluating your personal and community culture using the Cultural Values Continuum in appendix A. This will be key to self- and community awareness.

- If you were to introduce a new form of worship to your congregation, what would you say or do to introduce that new form?

- Consider the preaching, prayers, songs and other elements of your worship service. What is being formed in your congregation? What's not being formed?

Prayer: Thank you for your presence in each season of the church, Lord. Dwell in us, Holy Spirit, and help us to reflect on ways we open or close our arms to people of different backgrounds.

- *three* -

FOOD FIGHTS

Reconciliation in Worship

Planning a wedding is no easy task. Planning a crosscultural wedding in which everyone feels welcomed is almost a miracle. Having counseled crosscultural couples and planned for and officiated at their weddings, I think this might be an understatement. When my husband and I planned our wedding, we had many things to consider while attempting to meld two cultures, including communities from various racial backgrounds. We had decisions to make that would affect the ability for certain people to feel welcome. Language issues alone had the potential to alienate. If we had the wedding in English, family that traveled from afar would be left out. If it were in Spanish, a majority of our guests (white, black and Asian) would not be able to participate. Which language was more appropriate for our vows? Should we translate all of it live or have written translation? Though our parents did not weigh in, the stress was tremendous. Then there was the music. Will the ceremony flow if we have a gospel choir, a worship band, a string quartet and an organ? We wanted all four because the musicians involved were significant in our faith and artistic journeys.

We also considered the symbolic aspects of the wedding. We had observed a unity candle in some of our friends' weddings. In our African American friends' weddings we experienced jumping of the broom.[1] And in Latino and Filipino weddings we had witnessed El Lazo.[2] In Colombian weddings Las Arras are a focal point.[3] Once we chose the elements of the actual wedding service, we had to address the bigger cultural issue: time-oriented and event-oriented families. Should we send two different invitations, one with an 11 a.m. starting time and one with 10 a.m.? How were we going to clear out the chapel in time for the next wedding without offending our guests? Even the quantity of people was culturally based. My mother-in-law told my husband to have a small wedding and invite only immediate family and the closest of friends. While well-intentioned, this would not communicate love to all of my extended South American family in the United States.

After the wedding planning came the reception details and a new set of decisions to make. Should we serve alcohol or not? How do we have fun dance music in English, Spanish and Hindi while ensuring no lyrics cause offense? Will our non-Latin American friends and family feel ostracized by some salsa on the dance floor? Do we have food representative of our cultures? What if the reception hall couldn't cook Polish pierogies? And in all this, how is Christ reflected in our union?

The whole experience was wonderful. Our service did have organ, strings, diverse worship and a gospel choir. Our reception had Colombian appetizers, endless Argentine wine, swing dancing, Polish polka, salsa music and the dollar dance.[4] Everyone celebrated, and the dance floor was not segregated. Most of our friends expressed to us that the wedding was a great melding of communities and the most diverse guest list they had ever seen. We were so thrilled because we strived to be inclusive. We wanted our family and friends (Christian and non-Christian) to see our passion for reconciliation embodied.

COME, FOR EVERYTHING IS NOW READY

In Luke 14 we see another party that embodies reconciliation. The story is about a peculiar master. This master invites everyone to the table, and those who come must be willing to eat together.

> When one of those at the table with him heard this, he said to Jesus, "Blessed is the one who will eat at the feast in the kingdom of God."
>
> Jesus replied: "A certain man was preparing a great banquet and invited many guests. At the time of the banquet he sent his servant to tell those who had been invited, 'Come, for everything is now ready.'
>
> "But they all alike began to make excuses. The first said, 'I have just bought a field, and I must go and see it. Please excuse me.'
>
> "Another said, 'I have just bought five yoke of oxen, and I'm on my way to try them out. Please excuse me.'
>
> "Still another said, 'I just got married, so I can't come.'
>
> "The servant came back and reported this to his master. Then the owner of the house became angry and ordered his servant, 'Go out quickly into the streets and alleys of the town and bring in the poor, the crippled, the blind and the lame.'
>
> "'Sir,' the servant said, 'what you ordered has been done, but there is still room.'
>
> "Then the master told his servant, 'Go out to the roads and country lanes and compel them to come in, so that my house will be full. I tell you, not one of those who were invited will get a taste of my banquet.'" (Luke 14:15-24)

This story illustrates that the nature of the master is to extend hospitality to all, including those we wish he had not invited. The seemingly worthy guests who declined must have known the nature of this master and excused themselves from having to participate in this type of party where the "unworthy" might be present.

When the master announced through his servant, "Come, for everything is now ready," he was not sending an initial invitation. In that culture, parties last a long time and take days to prepare, so the guests would have known in advance. The master didn't have deep freezers for his steaks, and when an entire village is invited, that is a lot of meat. The guests had RSVPed to attend the banquet. Now, the food has been cooked, and the guests offer excuses for not coming. The excuses they offered were used to intentionally insult the master.[5] In Middle Eastern culture this would have been a powerful social message shaming and attacking the honor of the one hosting the party.[6]

Some commentators argue that the people did not want to attend the party because they were preoccupied with other things. The scene in the Near Eastern context, however, suggests that the excuses were not reasonable. The guests that declined had plenty of time to bow out. So, why did they offer these excuses? Not because they were busy.

The first excuse, "I have just bought a field, and I must go and see it," would have been ridiculous in a desert climate, where there is so little agricultural land. The land would already have been inspected before it was purchased. The second excuse, "I have just bought five yoke of oxen, and I'm on my way to try them out," is even more offensive than the first. Everyone would have known that a pair of oxen were useless if they did not walk together. Clearly this person had tested the oxen before he put a bid out. The third excuse is the most offensive of all.[7] Ken Bailey observes,

> The third man's excuse is unspeakably offensive. He says that (1) he has married a wife and (2) therefore he cannot come. He does not even ask to be excused. Middle Eastern chivalry

produces a dignified and respectful manner of talking about one's wife. This third guest is very rudely saying, "I have a woman in the back of the house, and I am busy with her. Don't expect me at your banquet. I am not coming."...

This guest will be home that night. His excuse is extremely rude and totally unacceptable. Ibn al-Tayyib comments on the three excuses by saying, "Here the master of the house became angry because he knew that the excuses were vain and the apologies were insults that demonstrated the hatred of the guests [for the house owner]."[8]

The nature of the master was clear to the guests, and they had no intentions of honoring him by attending the party. In fact, they wanted to close the party down. Bailey says, "If only one guest backs out, the banquet can proceed. But if there is collusion between the guests and they all withdraw, it will be clear that the guests intend to shut down the banquet."[9]

The servant also knew the master's nature and intentions to have everyone at his table. His invitation was for those with wealth *and* for those despised and marginalized by society. When the master told him to invite those on the outside, the servant's reply was, "What you ordered has been done." That is significant, because this passage is sometimes misinterpreted to mean that the master's second choice was those on the margins. As if he *prefers* certain guests but doesn't want the feast to go to waste so he *allows* those on margins of society to come in. Are the poor second choice? No! The poor and the outcast were on the guest list. What kind of master invites people on the margins? The kind that upsets the status quo and instigates revolution through relationship.

Jesus likewise instigates a revolution through reconciled relationships. Jesus calls his people to not only come and dine with him but to willingly dine with his other guests as well. Surprise! They might be people we'd rather not hang out with. Jesus does not ask the outcast and marginalized to come in the back door and sit in a certain section of the party. He extends hospitality to all and invites them into solidarity and mutuality at the table.

The table etiquette of the Jews, which was full of extra rules and regulations that caused divisions, did not come from the Lord. A meal was never just a meal. It was soaked in meaning about social status. The interactions and seating arrangements would indicate who was in or out, and first or last. Specifically in the book of Luke, Jesus is seen crossing socioeconomic boundaries at and around the table (see, for example, Luke 7). It's as if Jesus has picked the place of significance, the great banquet, to make a statement about the nature of eschatological kingdom banquet, which centers on a table of "ultimate blessing and belonging."[10] Later he says to his disciples,

> Who is greater, the one who is at the table or the one who serves? Is it not the one who is at the table? But I am among you as one who serves. You are those who have stood by me in my trials. And I confer on you a kingdom, just as my Father conferred one on me, so that you may eat and drink at my table in my kingdom and sit on thrones, judging the twelve tribes of Israel. (Luke 22:27-30)

Jesus' table not only crosses boundaries but redefines them. Outsiders are in, the down are up and the least are great. This is often called the "great reversal," rooted in Luke 13:30, where Jesus says, "Indeed there are those who are last who will be first, and first who will be last."

Getting people to gather at the table is symbolic of communion. At his last meal Christ broke bread, poured wine and instructed the disciples to remember his life and death through sharing a meal and remembering his body and blood. This act, also known as Communion, the Lord's Supper or Eucharist, is the centerpiece of worship.[11] The celebration of the Table has been central since the beginning of the Christian church. The Table therefore is a symbol of our gathering together for worship. Church historian Justo González states, "The center of worship was communion. This may be seen in the descriptions of the life of the church in Acts 2:46-47, where Luke tells us that 'Day by day, as they spent much time together in the temple, they broke bread at home and ate their food with glad and generous hearts, praising God.'"[12] González shows this breaking of bread is also repeated in Luke 20 and in the words of institution in 1 Corinthians 11, where Paul spends time instructing the believers about the celebration of the Lord's Supper. González closes by stating that worship in the early church was "centered in the breaking of bread."[13] At this Table all are welcome to come and meet with Christ and his family regardless of social status, gender or ethnic background.

Reconciliation

The parable in Luke 14 confirms two truths we find in other passages of Scripture. First, God calls all people to himself. Second, God calls his people to one another. So if you're at the table, you're one family. Following are some passages from the New Testament that reference the work of Christ in reconciliation.

God calls all people to himself.

All this is from God, who reconciled us to himself through Christ and gave us the ministry of reconciliation: that God was reconciling the world to himself in Christ, not counting people's sins against them. And he has committed to us the message of reconciliation. We are therefore Christ's ambassadors, as though God were making his appeal through us. We implore you on Christ's behalf: Be reconciled to God. (2 Corinthians 5:18-20)

God was pleased . . . through [Christ] to reconcile to himself all things. . . . Once you were alienated from God and were enemies in your minds because of your evil behavior. But now he has reconciled you by Christ's physical body through death to present you holy in his sight, without blemish and free from accusation. (Colossians 1:19-22)

The gospel . . . is the power of God that brings salvation to everyone who believes: first to the Jew, then to the Gentile. For in the gospel the righteousness of God is revealed—a righteousness that is by faith. (Romans 1:16-17).

God calls his people to one another.

He himself is our peace, who has made the two groups one and has destroyed the barrier, the dividing wall of hostility, by setting aside in his flesh the law with its commands and regulations. His purpose was to create in himself one new humanity out of the two, thus making peace, and in one body to reconcile both of them to God through the cross, by which he put to death their hostility. (Ephesians 2:14-16)

I now realize how true it is that God does not show favoritism but accepts from every nation the one who fears him and does what is right. (Acts 10:34-35)

[Let] there be no divisions among you, but that you be perfectly united in mind and thought. (1 Corinthians 1:10)

Reconciliation is central to and a mandate of the gospel. In worship we celebrate that "God was reconciling the world to himself in Christ," and we practice reconciliation as "Christ's ambassadors" (2 Corinthians 5:19-20). Reconciliation is not something we add to our worship; it is a practice in which we live out our true nature as one new humanity. Reconciliation and worship interconnect in striking ways. Worship, or adoration and exaltation of God in all his glory, is shown in the way that we live and love.

Reconciliation in worship is expressed in three ways: hospitality, solidarity and mutuality. This biblical reconciliation therefore calls us to welcome one another, stand with one another and depend on one another. Through congregational worship we can and should communicate: "I welcome you." "I am with you." "I need you." Professors Brenda Salter McNeil and Rick Richardson join worship and reconciliation by saying,

> It takes the Holy Spirit to melt down the inner barriers we have erected and to create in us a desire for God and for other people. . . . Worship is the power that opens us up to the possibility of reconciliation. It fosters an atmosphere of openness, vulnerability and humility that awakens us to what theologian Walter Brueggemann calls the "prophetic imagination." In worship we develop a vision of how God intends the world to be.[14]

HOSPITALITY

Leading worship in a multiethnic church is never boring, because we are innovating and creating new expressions in our given worship context. After the worship service, people often want to talk with the leader in response to what they experienced. I am never sure if the comments will be negative or positive, but I always brace myself for the unexpected. One morning a man quickly made his way to me and reached out for my forearm. With a smile from ear to ear he repeatedly thanked me for leading a song in Spanish. He told me that this was going to be their last Sunday at our church because his wife, being from Mexico, didn't feel at home in our church. He went on to express how tears flowed from her eyes as she sang in her own language and how meaningful it was for him to see her connect. He gestured to his wife, who came up behind him and grabbed me and gave me a huge hug. "This was going to be my last week, unless I heard from God. When you started the canción en Español, I knew it was a sign that we could make a home here." That was eight years ago, and they are now leaders in the congregation. Sarita, like most of us, was looking for a place where hospitality is experienced in worship.

Congregations typically do not adapt their worship to represent minority communities. The Association of Religion Data Archives reports that "the general pattern for multiracial congregations is to attempt to assimilate members of other racial groups into a congregational way of life established by the dominant racial group."[15] As someone who has led in multiracial communities, I have seen this phenomenon in action many times. Congregants from underrepresented communities typically learn what kind of multiethnic community it is (white-Asian, black-white, pan-Asian, Latino-black) and adapt to the expectation of the dominant culture. They are more like a visitor than an actual stakeholder in the community. It therefore should not surprise us that "members of the minority racial group in a congregation were significantly less likely to feel a sense of belonging, to have close friends in the congregations."[16]

As long as our worship makes people feel excluded or in constant visitor status, we are not accomplishing the ministry of biblical hospitality. When someone hosts a dinner at his or her house, the host controls the table. The guests relinquish control.[17] However, when we are creating an inclusive table in which there is room for all, the meal and experience will represent all who sit at the table. Otherwise, we are in effect saying, "Salad is served here; that is what we like. We love having you here, but please don't try to change us. Salad is really the best food for you. No substitutions allowed." In a multiethnic community no members should be made to feel like perpetual guests.

Reconciliation occurs when we get rid of all favoritism in our communities. That is difficult in settings that are similar culturally and socioeconomically, but imagine how much more our preferences are accentuated when different "smells" enter our places of worship. Once, while eating lunch in the café of a Christian college, I heard some students speaking poorly of the new foods that appeared in the refrigerator shared by all of the students. They spoke loudly in the presence of gentlemen from the ethnic group that the food represented. Not only were their comments generally offensive, but as younger white males they had no idea how their comments affected the older, more experienced pastor students in the room. It was not their intent to offend, but the impact was no less offensive. The church of the future must make space in our refrigerators.

It is beautiful when we allow ourselves to taste and see that the Lord is good through the gifts he gives us through others. As a Latina minister working with Asian, white and black students I constantly tried to get them to sing in Spanish. They reluctantly went along with me, and slowly began to receive the blessing of connecting with God in new ways. One weekend while at a conference, a group of students decided to have a spontaneous time of worship in the hallway of the hotel. There was no sound system, no screen and no lyrics. The guitar was passed from person to person as they each took turns leading in song. Tom, a Chinese American student, began to sing, "Aleluya, Aleluya, Mi alabanza sube a Ti."[18] The other students joined in with him, adding beautiful harmonies. It was a powerful moment for the students. The next morning their campus minister shared the following story with all the volunteers:

> I brought two students from a college I have been trying
> to build trust with. I was frankly very nervous about them

coming to the conference because although it is very diverse, there are few Latinos. They were walking around last night, and as they came down the escalator they heard a song in their own language (an Acts 2 moment). They did not see anything but followed the sound to encounter a group of Asian students singing in other tongues— Spanish. They were so surprised they were singing, without lyrics, and really worshiping. My students joined them and continued to worship. This morning, with tears in their eyes, they told me that they knew InterVarsity was a movement for them.

Worshiping in Spanish was forming my students as well as communicating welcome to other students who were looking for a place to belong. How might we communicate welcome to others in worship?

SOLIDARITY

Quest Church of Seattle is a multiethnic church of nine hundred primarily composed of Asian American and white congregants. They are committed to soul, community, reconciliation, compassion, justice and a global presence. While their church is only about 15 percent Latino and African American, they are committed to walking in solidarity with one another. They have an annual "faith and race" class, and interweave the issues of the world into their worship experiences. Quest regularly incorporates global lament during the pastoral prayer portion of worship. They spend time naming the global realities and standing with the communities in prayer. One Sunday evening they hosted a special event focusing on the 270 Nigerian schoolgirls kidnapped by Boko Haram terrorists on April 14, 2014. Quest leaders invited people to a prayer space with prompts toward lament and protection.[19]

In reconciliation we change places with one another to see the world through others' perspectives. The words *reconciliation* and *exchange* share the same root (e.g., money being exchanged in equal value). In reconciliation we exchange perspectives or change places. Worship provides the opportunity to stand with one another—to be reconciled. A mutual experience at the table exposes our ignorance about the world and others.

Solidarity means we identify with another's community in the practices of lament and joy; we join in empathetic grieving and rejoicing. This is not a new practice or idea; the Scriptures clearly call us to solidarity. Reflect on the following passages and imagine congregational worship that lives into this reality of solidarity:

> Care for one another. If one member suffers, all suffer together; if one member is honored, all rejoice together. (1 Corinthians 12:25-26 ESV)

> Carry each other's burdens, and in this way you will fulfill the law of Christ. (Galatians 6:2)

We stand with one another, as communities and individuals, in lament that leads to hope. We rejoice with one another when we see glimpses of the power of the gospel transforming situations. In solidarity we hope for this coming reality:

> Then I saw "a new heaven and a new earth," for the first heaven and the first earth had passed away, and there was no longer any sea. I saw the Holy City, the new Jerusalem, coming down out of heaven from God, prepared as a bride beautifully dressed for her husband. And I heard a loud voice from the throne saying, "Look! God's dwelling place is now among the people, and he will dwell with them. They will be his people, and God himself will be with them and be their God. 'He will wipe every tear from their eyes. There will be

no more death' or mourning or crying or pain, for the old order of things has passed away."

He who was seated on the throne said, "I am making everything new!" (Revelation 21:1-5)

This type of solidarity in worship transports us from the reality of the not yet. It reminds us of the kingdom to come. We can envision a place where we all as one body draw in closer to the glory of our God.

At a worship gathering of global leaders we worshiped to a song called "Magdan Lik," which was given to us by some of my friends at St. Samaans Church, also known as the Cave Church in the Mokattam (Garbage City), just outside Cairo, Egypt.[20] This community undergoes tremendous persecution as a religiously and socioeconomically marginalized community. The faith I saw them exhibit under difficult conditions was grounded in their legacy story of Simon the Tanner, who moved to Mokattam mountain in prayer. In English, the words of the song say,

> I proclaim that Jesus is the only King of my life.
> My heart is singing to Christ.
> With the sound of praises will I be a witness to Him.
> And my prayers will be heard.
> All my life, and my goals are for Jesus.
> And till He comes back, I will wait to see him in His glory.
> I sing joyful "Glory to you." Halleluiah.

Choosing that song was significant to me for a couple of reasons. First, I had been profoundly changed by my partnership with Egyptian Coptic Christians, and I wanted to expose American Christians to their depth of faith and compassion. Second, I wanted the participants to hear the Arabic language being used to worship Jesus. Too often we associate certain sounds, rhythms and images as being un-Christian, when they are merely un-Western. Hearing the language and rhythms, and seeing the Arabic characters on the screen, was a teaching moment for many attendees and a healing moment for many Arabic speakers who felt alienated by the American church. Years later I still receive emails, such as the following, thanking me for sharing that gift in such a public way:

> As a multiracial Lebanese, Italian, and German woman—I was hugely impacted by worshipping to Magdan Lik, since it was the first time I had ever sung a song in Arabic. It made me feel connected to my Lebanese/Middle Eastern culture in a way I had never before. It was very much the start of a slow journey in owning my Middle Eastern heritage. When I read the portion in your book (*The Mission of Worship*) as you described the audience singing that song, I was moved to tears to know that God had spoken to you about that song. I wanted thank you for your obedience to the Lord—almost 5 years ago in that moment and say that the song still has a powerful impact on me.

Worship is a way of connecting our lives with the lives of Christians in a completely different context in order to learn what it might be like to tell God "All my life is yours" in the midst of persecution and poverty.

Solidarity means we stand with one another in the practices of repentance and forgiveness. Reconciliation isn't accomplished at a conference or in a statement of intent. Biblical reconciliation requires consistently turning away from our participation in evil and repenting of the ways we wrong others. It also requires that we forgive those who have wronged us. Reflect on the following passages and imagine congregational worship that lives into repentance and forgiveness:

Be at peace among yourselves. . . . See that no one repays anyone evil for evil, but always seek to do good to one another and to everyone. Rejoice always. (1 Thessalonians 5:13-16 ESV)

Do not repay anyone evil for evil. . . .

"If your enemy is hungry feed him;
   if he is thirsty, give him something to drink. . . ."

Do not be overcome by evil, but overcome evil with good.
   (Romans 12:17-21)

When Christians reflect on current events, it is evident that we have strikingly different perspectives based on our cultural and social location.[21] Our reaction to racism in our country reveals how polarizing our viewpoints can be. We stand not with one another but on opposite sides. To see this we can examine the archives of *Christianity Today* or any generally Christian blog and view the comments posted on articles written on race and ethnicity in the church. It's fantastically horrible to see how Christians treat one another across those differences. When there were multiple deaths of black youth by white police officers, African American church leaders called people to pray and protest. Sadly, the movement continued to stay predominantly black. Black leaders requested white churches and white Christians to join them in solidarity. They asked them to listen and join together in prayer and lament. They asked them to intercede and march with them in solidarity. They asked, asked and asked. I was incredibly discouraged by the lack of response from white, Asian and Latino evangelical congregations, who continued church as normal Sunday after Sunday. I was discouraged by the lack of awareness white, Asian and Latino evangelicals had of the African American lament. On the flip side I was encouraged by young leaders of Evangelicals4Justice (#evangelicals4justice) in each of these communities, who not only prayed and protested in solidarity with black churches but informed and invited their friends and congregants to join them in the Black Lives Matter movement (#blacklivesmatter).

A post on Advent by Shannon Jammal-Hollemans, team leader for Faith Formation (CRC), captures beautifully the biblical call to solidarity and reconciliation:

> The face of God is most visible in our reconciliation, in the embrace of those whom we have wronged, in committing to love those who have harmed us when we surrender to God's purposes and the power of the Holy Spirit to work in our lives. I have seen the reconciling power of God's grace in the faces of pastors marching on the streets of Ferguson, Missouri. In tweets and posts on white privilege, and those who have committed to doing more than tweeting and posting about it. In the words and advocacy of those who desire to end the cradle to prison pipeline in so many of our nation's black communities. I have seen God most clearly in the places where the light of God's love has broken through via the mouths and hands and feet of God's people.[22]

Solidarity is not just a feeling; it can and should be practiced through word and deed. It should be practiced as we stand with one another in protest against injustice. It should be practiced through repentance and forgiveness. Worship can and should be a catalyst. These catalytic events can often be painful but powerful.

During a particularly deep time of grief in the African American community, one predominantly Latino church had a prayer service in which they practiced lament and intercession. Led by the black leaders of the church, they used candles, lights, artwork, music and prayer to help the congregation stand with their brothers and sisters of their community and country. It was a powerful time that led to many conversations about Latinos' racist attitudes toward African Americans, and the pain and sorrow that Latinos often feel when their pain is overlooked. This experience did not cause problems; it surfaced feelings that needed to be expressed.[23] It led to repentance and forgiveness.

I was asked to speak at a reconciliation-themed chapel at a predominantly white Christian university.[24] This was right after an incident in which the student body had sent offensive messages on social media regarding a recent chapel planned by students of color. The students had planned a beautiful service with elements from their churches. One of the elements was a mime troupe.[25] In response, one of the messages jokingly asked if this was "White face"![26] At its worst, this is blatant racism. At its best, it is a combination of ignorance and a failure to receive differences. Regardless of the intention, the impact was an act of exclusion and disrespect to people of color. To make things worse, a majority of the students on campus did not see it as a racial incident. They thought it was people freely expressing their opinions. The event was very painful, but it provided two lasting gifts. First, it exposed the façade that when Christians are in the same space, they are reconciled. Second, it moved the students to deeper dialogue on race and privilege. They had never been standing *with* one another; they simply stood *next to* each other.

Mutuality

Hospitality and solidarity lead to mutuality. First we say, "We welcome you." Then, "We stand with you." In mutuality we say, "We need you." Engaging in each other's forms of worship, and worshiping together across differences, leads us to a deeper place of dependence. In the example of the Christian university, the white students had no idea they were carrying a dislike for the unfamiliar and an attitude of entitlement that made them feel they could publicly wound their brothers and sisters. We need one another to expose our ignorance and racism. We also need each other for the various gifts our communities offer. When we honor the other, we display both the unity and the diversity of the church. As we learn from and receive gifts in worship from one another, we communicate, "We need you." Passages such as 1 Corinthians 12 and images from Revelation teach that we all contribute something substantial. *We* does not refer to individuals alone but to communities as well.

Those in crosscultural marriages find out how much they need each other. I once asked Karl if he wanted soup for dinner. He looked at me like I had landed from Mars. "Soup?" I asked, "Do you want soup for dinner?" He continued to stare and then responded, "Soup for dinner?" I didn't understand why he was puzzled. It's not like I asked him if he wanted to have breakfast for dinner (which apparently white Americans do occasionally). "Soup is not a dinner." I still made him a Colombian sancocho, a hearty soup that is more than a meal. He was imagining Campbell's chicken noodle or beer cheese soup, since he is from Wisconsin, where soup is a side dish. He regularly refers to this story when people ask what he enjoys about interracial marriage.

I learn something new about the worship and mission of God each time I collaborate with new communities. Recently I gathered a team of leaders from three different continents. A few leaders suggested a popular song from their region's movement that included the word *militant*. The song was written to honor students that were killed during protests in the streets, and the message of the song says, "I am a militant! I'm not afraid of battle, because my army is victorious and Jesus is Lord. Although it seems that there is no reason to keep fighting, I will not give up. I know that in the end the enemy will be defeated." I was not sure what to do with the song given that military or war images can be off-putting to Western Christians. I reached out to a few leaders from different countries for advice. Someone from the same region as those who suggested the song responded that the song is very important to them because of their political and economic history. She reminded me that Western Christians need to learn from movements that have experienced being a witness in the midst of opposition, such as in Africa, Asia and Latin America. Another leader who is American but works globally said,

> In America, we don't personally experience a lot of war and maybe we need to be exposed. However, for others, I suspect the issue of war, not so much the word "militant," might provoke some emotion (pain, anger, political pride) especially in some places that are still suffering from grief displacement, such as Ukraine, the Middle East and Northern Africa. There are also the more recent Kenya college student murders where Islamic extremists intentionally sought out Christian students to kill them if they could not recite their (Islamic) beliefs. Kenya is striving for peace, healing and wholeness, so I wonder if using war and army imagery might be difficult.

There was an opportunity to help nations worship together, but we had to do some educating on the meaning and importance of the song, as well as some empathizing with others. We had to be prepared for emotional feedback and provide space for healing prayer. To adopt a more prophetic stance toward mutuality we were willing to take risks in order to see what work the Holy Spirit could do in this situation.

Many people ask me why they should do multiethnic worship when everyone in their church is from the same background. My answer: "Even if you don't have any _____ [insert group], you still need to learn from their encounters with God. It's not just for them; it's for you." The first time I heard Kari Jobe sing "Revelation Song" (by Jennie Lee Riddle), I saw how this beautiful beloved community would look. I closed my eyes as I listened, but I didn't hear English. The words and biblical image required a rearrangement of the song to include the voices of my friends, and the lovely chaos of overlapping harmonies and languages. I hope we will see these types of communities on earth as it is in heaven. This motivates me to work with communities to develop spaces of worship that are a foretaste of the kingdom in its fullness. Can you imagine it?

Holy, Holy, Holy is the Lord God Almighty,
who was and is and is to come.

Santo, santo, santo, Dios todopoderoso
Quien fue, quien es y quien vendrá

Saint, oui saint, trois fois saint, Est le Seigneur tout-puissant
Qui est, qui était et qui revient,

聖哉, 聖哉, 聖哉,
全歸主至聖全能
昨今不變亦永不變

Hospitality. "We welcome you." Inclusive worship services for underrepresented.

Solidarity. "We stand with you." Prayer and song that affirm unity around major events in community and world.

Mutuality. "We need you." Being led by one another.

Conclusion. Reconciliation should inform and shape our worship. Leading worship in a multiethnic world requires extending hospitality in ways the church historically has not done. Our desire to include others and embrace them for who they are is communicated in our worship practices. If biblical reconciliation calls us to welcome one another, stand with one another and depend on one another, how are we communicating this through congregational worship?

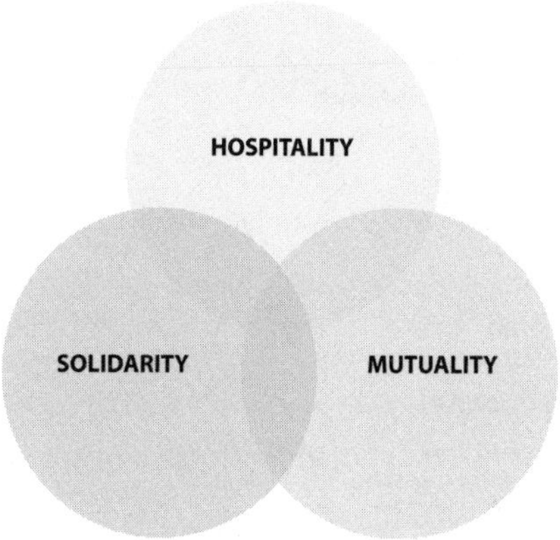

Figure 3.1

The following are ways to grow personally in this area.

- Start with your relationships. Do you know Christians from other cultural backgrounds? If so, learn from them. Ask them about their church experiences (sermons, baptisms, Lord's Supper, praise and worship).

- Visit a church of a different ethnic background with your family. Start with friendships with or connections to a different ethnic group via denominational ties or a missions trip.

- Practice personally. Learn a worship song from one of your friends or church visits, and use it in prayer. Check out some of the following resources to learn songs:
    - o Urbana Missions Conference CDs
    - o Proskuneo
    - o Sacred Roots

- Share with your church members and worship pastor what you have been learning from your experience.

- Read books on reconciliation (see appendix B).

KEY CONCEPTS

- God reconciles people to himself and to one another.
- Jesus invites all to the Table, which is a center of worship.
- Reconciliation is expressed in hospitality, solidarity and mutuality.

FOR REFLECTION

- In what ways do you need the gifts of the diverse body of Christ? What have you done to pursue influence by others? What keeps you from growing in this area?
- How is your worship intentionally communicating "We welcome you," "We stand with you," and "We need you"? What might that look like in your context?
- Identify relationships of solidarity and mutuality with people from other cultures that you can draw from to deepen your worship. How can you grow in those? What's keeping you from them?

FOR DISCUSSION

- How can your worship help others trade places with one another?
- Are there people with whom you or your congregation would rather not be reconciled? Why is that, and how can you utilize your worship to draw your fellowship into reconciliation?

Prayer: Lord, help me to live out your call to reconciliation in hospitality, solidarity and mutuality. May your Spirit fill my community as we worship with your global church.

- four -

HOSTING WELL

Shared Leadership

It all went down over a cup of cafecito (literally "little coffee"). John and I had this heart-to-heart coming for a long time. For many years John had been a musician and worship leader for a large suburban church, and had a good reputation as a worship leader in the area. We met while collaborating in a multiethnic ministry as I coached him and exposed him to new ideas and approaches to worship and worship leading. Now, John had received an invitation to teach on multicultural worship at a conference. He thought it would be great to have my voice on his panel. What a reversal! I had been practicing, teaching and training in diverse worship for almost a decade. He has been learning for nine months. But I was supposed to sit on his panel?

This led us to a series of conversations about how gender, race and power play out in the church. What he thought would be an honoring invitation was offensive to me! Why was he leading this seminar and not someone like myself? Why was he at the table and not one who had experience? Privilege! I asked him flat out if having diverse voices at the table was important. His response was

"Yes, but if there is only one spot at the table, I still want to be there. I am not ready to give that up." My head all but exploded as I said, "You want to reserve your space at that table to speak into something you know little about; you still feel entitled to that spot. And it does not bother you one bit that there is no one like myself— female or person of color—at a table full of white men acting as experts on diversity in worship?" After we exchanged many words and tears, he confessed that in his circles worship leaders in his position were rock stars! He had never seen anyone give up that status, and he was not sure how to do that and still fulfill his call. It makes sense from his perspective. Why share his space? No one else was. Handing over leadership to others is rarely practiced.

ROCK STARS: A MAN, A PLAN AND A GUITAR

Worship leaders are treated like rock stars! They hold their guitar or microphone and become the center of our attention. We follow them in flocks. We pay $50 to $100 to hear them in concert. We spend thousands to travel to conferences where they are featured. We spend even more acquiring their songs so that we can consume them at our leisure. Particularly in a culture that is perpetuating the rock-star worship leader, why would we share our leadership? And how do we do it? Very few of us have seen it done, especially by the American-worship idols who have captured our attention and dollars. We don't expect it, we can't envision it and no one has taught us how to share. The very position that is supposed to help people enter into the presence of the self-sacrificing God ends up fostering ego battles. Ironically, a priestly role actually lends itself to creating idols.

A cookbook that many of my bachelor friends use, *A Man, a Can, a Plan*, encourages men to successfully cook on their own as long as they have cans of food.[1] In worship we have this same phenomenon, but its called "A Man, a Plan and a Guitar." While they might not suffer from rock-star syndrome, these worship leaders sit in their office Tuesday through Thursday and listen to music, plan worship sets and develop their own liturgy. You may be thinking, *What's wrong with that? Why shouldn't I select all the songs and plan all the arrangements? It's my job as worship director, and I have the training and experience and took music theory in college. I know how it all works. More importantly, I work with volunteers. I have more time to do it than everybody else. Someone needs to be the point person and make the decisions, and it's my job to do that.* Our worship-planning models rarely require more than one person. And if worship is planned by a team, the team likely is not multicultural. This is by far the norm for worship planning that I've observed around the country.

Hosting a gathering of diverse people who can express and enjoy a variety of views requires collaboration. A friend was running for city council, and we wanted to ensure she received support from all facets of the community, which, due to gentrification and rising rental costs, was divided between older and newer residents. Dialogue between the groups was necessary, but who could draw both into a conversation with "others"? Friends from each group! Maria, a Latina, and Aaron, a hipster, gathered Hispanics and hipsters together to talk about the mounting tension. If only one had gathered friends and hosted the conversation, only people from his or her community would have come, and only one group's needs would have been met. Hosting the event together enabled Maria and Aaron to create an atmosphere conducive to both communities. Their partnership and shared leadership made it possible to gather people across differences and address the needs of both groups. They needed one another to host a successful conversation, and the gathering itself revealed that both parties *needed* one another for future success.

Collaboration requires sharing power, real power. It requires co-creation and co-decision making. Shared leadership invites us to empty ourselves of complete power or control. With words and actions it expresses "I need you." Collaboration requires community and a variety of gifts at the table. This is most clearly modeled in Christ's emptying himself of power and going to the cross (Philippians 2:5-8). Followers of Christ, those who take mutuality and community seriously, are invited to likewise empty ourselves. The biggest obstacle to giving up power and sharing a seat at the table is the inability to take risks. This aversion to taking risks is driven by fear, pride, control and self-doubt. Admitting need and choosing downward mobility by sharing power isn't a top priority.

We will not host well without collaborating with people from other communities. Unless we have a community of diverse leaders who can speak into the situation and co-create spaces, we will repeatedly go to our favorite foods, music, decorations and event-planning processes. Thus, people of different ethic, cultural, class and generational backgrounds will not feel fed. Leading worship in relevant, dynamic ways for the future of a diverse church depends on our ability to share leadership. It begins with an environment of mutual learning and collaboration in which worship-team participants can add value and perspective from their diverse traditions. This approach is distinctive in that it is not primarily about collecting songs and components from different traditions and assigning people from those traditions to lead (tokenism), but allowing the traditions of team members to shape the overall community and worship experience. In "Multicultural Congregations and Worship: A Literature Review" Terry York states that a congregation's invitation should be "not only 'sit here as an attendee,' but 'stand here as a contributor, a leader.'" Creating an environment of full participation in leadership and decision-making seems to be a key to any honest commitment to the project.[2]

Creating this environment starts with accepting the fundamental reality that all leaders have strong preferences, even about leadership, that are shaped by social and cultural location. Before talking about how to share, we need to look at three aspects of crosscultural leadership.

LEADERSHIP AND CULTURE

What is the purpose of the leadership? Missiologist James Plued-demann states, "The ultimate purpose of the leadership is to bring people into full relationship with their Creator. We are created to know, love and glorify God."[3] Beyond that, though, leadership style and practice are culturally located. Before we can look at how to share leadership, we need to understand the dynamics of leading, following and inviting crossculturally.

Leading crossculturally. What is the role of a leader? Is a leader's job to tell people where they are going (casting vision)? Is it to delegate tasks (manager)?

While having a conversation with a young African American gentleman about good leadership, he said that a good leader would tell his church, "This is the vision God has for us, and here's how we are going to get there." This, he said, would create a sense of security for the leaders under that pastor. I laughed because if I had ever done that with student leaders (particularly white students), I would have had an exodus on my hands. Millennials, especially those coming from places of privilege, do not want to be told what they are going to do and how to get there. That would be a huge turnoff and maybe would even set off alarms. So, who's right?

In an urban setting where there are many insecurities (safety, food, etc.), and family bonds are often broken due to housing, incarceration or long work hours, the community is looking for someone—a parish priest, influential schoolteacher or father figure—to provide stability. John Zayas, pastor of Grace and Peace Church in urban Chicago, says, "They want to know that someone knows what's going on!"[4] Expressions of leadership develop within the context of the leader and his or her followers. It is also anchored in values of hierarchy. The kind of leadership Pastor Zayas speaks of would be counterintuitive to my context as a campus minister equipping and mobilizing student leaders. The context or role I had was to delegate and coach them. The goal was not providing stability but opportunities to test and grow them into leadership.

These questions go back to issues of culture—not at the level of behavior but at the level of values. There are many ways to differentiate leadership values: egalitarian versus hierarchical, individualism versus collectivism, low context versus high context. (It may be worth going back to the cultural continuum in appendix A.) One helpful tool that I have used to help people consider leadership and culture comes from Plueddemann's *Leading Across Cultures*. He overlays Henry Blanchard's Situational Leadership Chart with crosscultural values to come up with a new Multicultural Situational Leadership Chart. Plueddemann states that expectations for leaders and followers should change in a crosscultural setting:

> Effective leaders will be flexible in their style by assessing the cultural expectations of leaders and followers. As the cultural situation changes so does the leadership style. Effective multicultural followers will also adapt their understanding and expectations as they serve under leaders with different cultural expectations. Both leaders and followers must be aware of the expectations of the host culture, adapting accordingly. Multicultural leaders and followers need to be proficient in a wide range of leadership styles, and know when to use which one.[5]

This resonates with my experience as someone who has fallen flat on her face so many times as both a leader and a follower. Imagine a bicultural Latina American working (1) under a Korean pastor, (2) leading Asian American and white young adults, (3) in China leading a missions trip or (4) as a congregant in a black church. Can you begin to imagine how many mistakes I have made? I always tell people that once we think we've got it down, God invites us to live and love a totally different segment of his people—just to keep us humble.

Imagine this scenario: A leader from a more egalitarian culture who values getting tasks accomplished is overseeing a group of younger people from a culture who value hierarchy and maintaining relationships. The leader believes it's his job to cast vision and set clear expectations, and assumes that people who have concerns, questions or disagreements will let him know so that they can be addressed. The followers, however, feel it's inappropriate to question the older leader, especially in public. The leader lays out plans for a worship set, including music, Scripture reading, spoken word and even wardrobe coordination. He asks the group what they think and expects collaboration. None is received.

What's the dynamic like after months of this scenario being played out? The leader is likely frustrated and feeling alone. Or perhaps the leader believes all is well. The participants are feeling neglected, even marginalized (see table 4.1).

Table 4.1. Crosscultural Leadership Misunderstandings

Leader	Followers
Focused on tasks; egalitarian	Value hierarchy and submission to elders
Asks for direct feedback in public	Feel they can't challenge a leader in front of others
Feels alone, frustrated or even that all is well	Feel neglected, marginalized

Following crossculturally. As followers we also have to do some deep reflection to identify how our culture is shaping our preferences. Researching for this book has provided many opportunities for owning up to my mistakes. Plueddemann states that in some cultures loyalty may be more valued than competency.[6] When I read this a light bulb went on. If it had been a literal light bulb, it could have given enough light to land a jumbo jet. His explanation shed light on a repeated conflict I had been having with a particular leader. I wanted to be valued for my competency. In order to support this leader and his ministry I would offer to preach, train leaders and organize job descriptions for the staff. He wanted my support, but in loyalty, not from my expertise. Ministry is hard, and he wanted to know people would protect him from critics and preserve his reputation when he made mistakes. In hindsight I think he must have mentioned loyalty about fifty times in the years I had known him. He referred to people's loyalty regularly and said he really needed to know people were loyal. I actually wondered why he was constantly questioning my loyalty, and I in turn, to show my support, worked harder so he knew he could count on me and my expertise. I wish I could say that I learned better, but in that cultural situation, I was a bad follower.

Inviting crossculturally. How do people become leaders? Do we invite people into leadership? Are they appointed? Do they apply? Do they volunteer or wait to be approached? I was at a small gathering of worship leaders trying to identify a leadership pipeline for the ministry. When I asked how the others identified leaders, a white male leader said, "We'll know who leaders are because they will step up." Interestingly, just weeks before in another conversation, a female colleague expressed her disappointment that she was regularly overlooked for a leadership summit that was by invitation only, and we lamented together. A male ministry partner then pointed out to me that the summit was by either application or nomination, not by nomination only. He wondered why she didn't apply. What was keeping my friend from applying? She was rehearsing cultural and social influences that were reinforced by her understanding of Scripture.[7] Luke 14:7-11 was in her head.

When he noticed how the guests picked the places of honor at the table, he told them this parable: "When someone invites you to a wedding feast, do not take the place of honor, for a person more distinguished than you may have been invited. If so, the host who invited both of you will come and say to you, 'Give this person your seat.' Then, humiliated, you will have to take the least important place. But when you are invited, take the lowest place, so that when your host comes, he will say to you, 'Friend, move up to a better place.' Then you will be honored in the presence of all the other guests. For all those who exalt themselves will be humbled, and those who humble themselves will be exalted."

Gender, ethnic or socioeconomic biases affect how we choose leaders. In his book on Asian American leadership Paul Tokanaga compares Asian American and dominant American behavior to highlight how Asian American behavior is often interpreted as lack of interest or lack of leadership skills.[8] He says, "In an Asian American gathering, it feels presumptuous, aggressive and even arrogant to raise a hand and say, 'I'll do it.' . . . What is called respect in one culture looks like apathy in another."[9] In some cultures leaders are applauded for stepping up; in others leaders disqualify themselves by assuming they can lead. They need a sponsor to invite them to lead. Some leaders I have worked with in my community are intimidated by wealth and education, and therefore do not see themselves as having something to contribute. As you share your leadership, consider that even your method of inviting others to the table has cultural elements at play.

I'm so grateful for all the training I've received in my adult life. I was taught strategic planning processes working with dominant-culture organizations who taught me to evaluate, develop vision and build strategy to accomplish that vision. I was instructed on making SMART goals (specific, measurable, attainable, relevant and time oriented). As a pastor in an urban context with Latinos and African Americans, I tried to lead my church staff and board though a similar planning process. I thought I had made allowances for the collective nature of the congregation as well as the flexibility needed for deadlines. I did not account for the high-context culture in which vision and strategy are more intuitive and spontaneous, and less precise and quantifiable. Years later I still am not always sure what our plan is, but that does not mean there isn't one. God is doing great things, and everyone seems to be onboard and knows what is happening. It is not a deficiency in my church but a difference in approach. This flexibility and ambiguity allows us to flow with the Spirit and respond to local issues, which in turn makes us effective in our context. Here again I thought I had crossed cultures, even within my own Latino-ness, but I had more to learn.

LEVELS (OR DEGREES) OF SHARED LEADERSHIP

Now that we have considered some foundational ways culture affects leadership, we can explore how we share leadership. The hallmark of a multiethnic worship team is that people from different backgrounds are given the authority to influence the shape of worship. In order to do that they may be required to learn about their particular community—their theology, style and story—alongside one another.

Planning collaboratively is a good practice for any church. In a lecture titled "Beyond Lone Ranger Leadership: People and Roles in the Worship Life of the Congregation," John Witvliet proposes the following points:

- Gathering a group of people to train and intentionally plan worship is helpful.

- Develop a good model for communication that supports your team.

- Steward the gifts given to the congregation or community you are involved in.

- Look for opportunities to develop leaders.[10]

In order to prepare effectively for the type of worship spaces we will need, the rock star will have to move aside for leaders who are willing to share space. Most people participating in the congregation may not be able to tell when the Latino singing the Spanish song is a form of tokenism or is an empowered member of the team. For most of the last decade diverse worship has been merely singing in different languages or having a multicolored team. This is what I remember when I first came on to the scene in 1995, but I hope that the depth and sophistication in the practice has grown beyond mere tokenism. I have been in churches where the worship at first glance looks similar to other multiethnic church worship, but when I look closer I notice that the singers are indeed more like musicians than leaders. Empowerment is not there.

Different levels of shared leadership are outlined in table 4.2. At their heart is the question of empowerment and participation to influence.

Table 4.2. Levels of Shared Worship Team Leadership

Type	Team	Songs/Planning	Leadership
Multiethnic music	homogeneous	diverse, chosen by director	director
Multiethnic team	diverse	diverse, chosen by director	director
Multiethnic shared singing	diverse	diverse, chosen by director	others sing but do not pastor
Multiethnic worship with team ownership	diverse	diverse, chosen by director	others pastor
Multiethnic worship with team leadership	diverse	diverse, chosen by small group or team	others pastor

The first two levels of shared leadership shown on table 4.2 are both "a man and a plan" leadership. In both cases we are likely looking at a team of professional musicians who can duplicate diverse styles of music but are taking their cues from one leader. These worship experiences do not invite the congregation into the *feel* of the worship culture. This reminds me of a choir conducted by someone classically trained. Though they're singing a South African song, the experience clearly is not South African, mostly due to the reserved movement of the choir. Maybe it's a gospel song, but the leader isn't truly ministering in that style.

In both of these first two levels it's likely that one worship director is shaping and leading the entire experience, which is a sort of potluck—one type of music from each ethnicity—or mostly contemporary Christian music with a few other elements thrown in. This is common in ethnically homogeneous churches trying to create an environment hospitable to newcomers. The worship leader may be interested in exploring diverse worship and begin to take risks in that direction even if people from other communities are not present on the worship team. The only variable between the first and second levels is that the team is multiethnic in the second.

In the third level, which is the most common model I have seen, the leader selects all of the songs in the song package used during the services. The leader also controls the arrangement of the song, vocals, dynamics and song form. After selecting and arranging the songs, the leader assigns someone (usually from the culture of the song) to a portion of or the whole song. This allows the person to sing, ad-lib along the way and *maybe* end the song as he or she sees fit, which likely means additional repetitions of the chorus with a variety of dynamics. As I stated earlier, this model is not very messy. The pastoral words and overall form of the song is led by the worship leader. The congregation will be blessed by a different sound, but not by different spiritual guidance, which remains the same.

This model does not allow the singer to pastor or guide the congregation. The singer was likely chosen for the sound and style of his or her voice, not for leadership capacity. This is also not helpful because the worship leader likely is not from that culture and may arrange the song in a counterintuitive way to the community it comes from. For example, in my early years I served on worship teams who selected Spanish songs for me to sing that were not well-known or were arranged in ways that would never be heard in a native Latino church. I would say, "Hola," sing my Spanish song and pray in Spanish. This level is helpful in a few cases: when training worship leaders (youth or newer leaders), when working with a new team and when a vocalist is a great worshiper but does not lead well.

The fourth level of leadership begins as the first does; the worship leader selects the songs and assigns the person(s) to lead in singing them. The person is likely chosen not for his or her sound or style but for the ability to pastor and guide the moment (celebration, reflection, repentance). This person's gifts will shine as he or she introduces the song via Scripture, words of exhortation or prayer. The singer shapes the form of the song and conducts the band from beginning to end. When the moment is finished, he or she passes leadership back to the worship leader (maybe with a nod).

The benefit of this increased leadership is that it allows for the moment of the song to be developed by the song leader, who is given authority. Therefore the congregation is experiencing true leadership. These moments are especially needed when training worship leaders in multiethnic worship. It is helpful for song selection to remain with the team leader when there are time crunches or when other stakeholders are giving opinions on service order and flow.

At the final level of leadership, all members of the team shape the worship. Different voices contribute to the selection of songs for the overall package. People who are leading a particular service are invited to choose their own songs, prayers and Scripture readings. If there are multiple leaders in a service, together they select from the songs the team has chosen. The team, or small group of leaders, also weighs in on the overall theme, tone and reason for the worship time. They shape the whole, but each executes only his or her part within that whole. They all know what they are doing and why.

This level of leadership takes an immense amount of emptying on the part of the worship leader. There is no room for pride, fear or control. This takes more time as well; the process is much more involved and requires trust in planning and synergy and chemistry in the service. The worship leader still takes ultimate responsibility for the time. If it fails, the team leader is responsible. If the experience and practice is a success, all team members share in the celebration for having shaped it. Who wants that job? Not many people, which is why this model is rarely practiced.

Ideally, our intent is to share as much as possible. This may not mean an equal voice for everyone. There may be a smaller group within the team that has more influence. Certain levels of influence and participation may not be appropriate for someone in training as a worship leader, or if someone does not have the capacity. Leaders may rotate week to week versus all being on the team each week. Sharing can happen many ways.

TOKENISM IS NOT AN OPTION

A few years back when I was collaborating with another worship director, I asked about the worship sets. He told me they were already posted on an online database. I asked how he already knew the song form if he had not spoken to the song leaders. He informed me that they would be following the song forms he had selected. "Oh, so they are not leading the song?" I asked. He responded, "No, as the director I choose the song form, and it stays the same regardless of who is leading the song and what set it goes in." "So, you're not really sharing your leadership?" I blurted out before I could shape the statement in a nicer way. After a moment of silence he told me that it gets messy when many people arrange songs, keys and forms, depending on who is leading it and when it is being used. He prefers to shape the entire liturgy himself and plug singers in based on how they sound.

This revealed that he ultimately saw himself as a producer and the sole spiritual leader of the experience. Choosing the singers was like selecting a trumpet versus a flute for a particular sound. Obviously, I had a disconnect with the philosophy and approach of this worship leader. Our definitions of *leader* differed. For him it meant *singer*. My approach is that within a set (four to five songs, prayers, readings, etc.) the person I delegate to lead will utilize the five to seven minutes to invite the congregation to join him or her in whatever manner he or she sees fit. During this time this leader has the place of authority. Yes, I agree—it is messy. It take an immense amount of trust to co-lead or share for a short amount of time (e.g., twenty-five to thirty minutes). It means the two leaders have discussed the liturgical moment and know what they are trying to help people attend to. They trust each other when changes are made to the plan.

Many pastors say they share leadership on their worship team, but in reality singers are used as instruments instead of for their leadership potential.

There are, however, multiethnic team models that employ high collaboration, inclusion and shared leadership. For these teams the root of a successful partnership is in both the planning and the worship practice. Collaboration and input from a variety of voices are needed. Sharing leadership is also important for marginalized voices to be heard and marginalized values to be contributed.

When the person in power in a multiethnic worship situation is normally in power elsewhere (generally white males), then sharing leadership feels especially costly, given that it is countercultural and the person has the most to empty. This trend is seen in multiethnic churches as well as multiethnic parachurch movements, where the leader of a successful diverse community is typically white and male. Given the leadership pipelines that are in place, people of color tend to be younger and newer to the ministries, therefore they rarely occupy places of significant leadership. And the team leader is most likely someone from an individualistic culture rather than collective one.

Leaders who share power model mutuality and reciprocity in prophetic ways to the North American church. This way of doing things models justice! It is not merely a multicolored group of musicians on the stage but a process in which people's cultural gifts and narratives are brought to the table.

WHY DON'T LEADERS SHARE?

Leadership is affected by our ego issues. Good leadership invites us to the cross and emptying, which release us to practice humility. As we've moved along, I've mentioned some of the reasons people do not share leadership. Recently, I asked a gathering of seasoned worship leaders who do empower others to articulate their own journey. Here are a few reasons sharing leadership does not happen, summarized from conversations and email responses.

Ego. Let's be real for a second! We like being the center of attention. Let's face it, we are artists who are motivated by the recognition of our unique artistic contribution. We are also performers. Hello? We actually thrive on being the center of attention and applauded for our gifts. That's where they get the phase "being in the spotlight." We are leaders, which means we each have a healthy level of confidence to believe people will follow us and go where we believe they should go. We have ideas, dreams and *big* plans in general. The fact that we submit them to God is a miracle in and of itself. But we need practices that help us die to self. When working with a team to select songs, that is why I clarify that they can't pick a song for our team merely because their voice sounds great on it. (This really does happen.)

Fear of failure or risk taking. The type of worship spaces we are creating are new. Those of us that work in prophetic ministries that ask questions about the future of worship are developing something that has not been done, and therefore we are aware that critique will come. When we hand over power to others and it does not go well, it reflects on us because ultimately we are responsible.

Control. We like to know the outcome and who better to ensure that than ourselves. When developing multiethnic worship it is likely that you are training leaders who are newer to crossing cultures. Many musicians will come confidently to participate but will confront their limitations as they practice multiethnic worship. Sometimes it's just easier to do it yourself. Their pronunciation will not always be as good as yours. They may not know how to deliver an introduction to a song that stylistically matches. Quality control is in your hands.

Inefficiency. Projects that have multiple stakeholders always take more time. You are in a constant feedback loop about what songs, which leaders and how to arrange music. You may also have times where it can be unclear who is making the final decision based on your structure. Collaboration takes more time, and may not be helpful given the timeline you have.

Pride/insecurity. What if I let them lead, and people like them more. The contributing team members that you will share leadership with may have better voices than you. They may be more gifted as pastors.

Self-sufficiency. Competent leaders do things on their own. They succeed, write a book on it and go on a speaking tour. If we are the "face" of quality crosscultural worship, we can make a career out of it. If we admit our need for one another, which leaders are often taught to hide, then we will have to share our glory. No speaking tour for us.

Whatever our reasons for not sharing leadership, we have to examine ourselves. Ask the Lord what is keeping you from inviting the gifts and narratives of others into worship. Consult with a friend on how you are doing in this area. Repent if the reason is that you merely enjoy the spotlight. The application here is simple. Empty yourself and make space for other people to serve with their gifts.

Matt Lundgren, worship director at Willow Creek Community Church in South Barrington, Illinois, is a close friend and fantastic pastor and musician. He is a humble leader with incredible battle scars. When I first met him, we were collaborating on some projects for a denomination, and I'm not going to lie, it was an awkward start. We had different ideas about leadership and worship. He had much more expertise as a musician than I, but I came with deep experience in multiethnic communities. He is a reminder to me that anyone can change, no matter how famous or gifted. I'd love you to hear his story of multiethnic worship in his own words:

> I'm the problem. You see, as a white guy I've had things handed to me on a silver platter most of my life. I haven't ever suffered from racial or gender discrimination—"the powers that be" always favored me. Without really being aware of it, God started doing some things in me to expand my cultural views. Through the process I realized, I had been preventing the minority cultures around me to worship God, and I was going to become the solution within my growing sphere of influence. I intentionally built deep friendships across racial lines, and I didn't just ask these friends to sing

or play along to the "white" rock music, but I would actually have them lead a song in Spanish or a gospel or hip-hop song. I looked at how far I had come in my own understanding of worship in a multicultural context, and I became very proud. And then, in the words of every single VH1 *Behind the Music* episode—"it all came crashing down." I realized that so long as a white guy was continually being asked to plan and lead, we were only going to get so far in our efforts of multicultural worship. I was ashamed to say that I am not the solution; I am the problem. Now, when I lead worship in a multicultural context, I am not the worship planner and leader, I am one of the worship planners. This journey of emptying has not been easy. There have been times when I offended other members of my team. There have been times when I would think to myself, *Why am I going to all this trouble? It would be so much easier if I just did it all myself.* It was those times that I would remind myself that I am the problem—that's why I am doing this. The result has been far greater than I ever could have possibly imagined. It's become the joke in my band now that the only reason I am in the band is because I'm the one who is getting the gigs; I don't even need to be on stage anymore—actually, they are probably better without me.[11]

KEY CONCEPTS

- Leadership style and practice are culturally located, so we must be knowledgeable of how that affects leadership selection and practice.

- Leading worship in relevant, dynamic ways for the future diverse church depends on our ability to share our leadership.

- Leadership should be shared to its fullest extent.

FOR REFLECTION

- Have you experienced leaders handing over their leadership reins to others? Why is this rarely practiced? Where have you seen it practiced?

- Does collaboration and input from a variety of voices appeal to you? Why? What about it scares you? What would be gained? What would be lost?

- As you think about your own leadership, what are some steps you can take toward collaboration?

- Describe how your culture views leadership. How is this different from those you lead or who lead you?

FOR DISCUSSION

- If you're a leader where there isn't much diversity, you could still do multiethnic worship and share your leadership. Who might you share it with? How might you expose yourself to influence from other leaders around the globe so your worship can become more diverse?

- Gather together with some worship leaders to discuss the reasons why leaders don't share their platform. Confess and ask forgiveness.

Prayer: Lord, help me to be honest with myself. In my leadership help me to be openhanded, to understand my need for others and to practice humility. May leaders be lifted up as a result of working with me. I pray that my community will be blessed as others' gifts shine.

- *five* -

DESIGNING YOUR MENU

Models of Diverse Worship

One holiday I was visiting with my in-laws and we decided to visit a church on their block for Christmas Eve. This church actually belonged to the denomination in which I pastor, so we were excited to worship with family. We were greeted outside by a gray-haired gentleman who led us into the building where we were handed a bulletin with the detailed order of service. Everyone was already seated; the service started six minutes prior to our arrival. The choir, accompanied by an organ, violins and a brass section, led us in traditional carols and hymns in four-part harmony. It was a powerful service of remembering the Christmas story through songs and Scripture. It was also an experience of cultural displacement that took me back to my university days singing in a vespers service chorale. I was so moved by the experience that I cried multiple times during the service and wanted to shout amen throughout the Scripture reading and short meditation by the pastor. (Don't worry, I knew that would not fly in this setting.)

On the way home from the service I debriefed the experience like I always do. (It's a work hazard.) I expressed how distinctive in almost every way this service was from the Christmas service in my church. I admitted I was glad to pull out my formal musical skills to sing in a more traditional style. I also confessed it would be hard to preach regularly in a community that did not communicate back to me while I was preaching. The whole way home I kept repeating, "Wow, culture really *does* impact how you express yourself in worship. It's just so different. I almost can't believe we are the same denomination." By the racial and ethnic makeup of the church it was obvious that we were not the same, and their worship practices gave clarity to that, as can be seen by the reviewing table 5.1. Take a few minutes to reflect on the comparison; what stands out to you? Remember neither one is better than the other, it's just a matter of preference for each of the different communities.

Table 5.1. Comparison of Two Christmas Eve Worship Experiences

	Latino Church	**White Church**
Greeting	Six greeters kiss or hug	One greeter shakes hand
Bulletin	Prayers; no service order	Detailed service order
Congregation	Predominantly Latino and black	Predominantly Dutch Americans
Style	Contemporary; intergenerational	Traditional; intergenerational
Music	Band	Choir, organ, brass
Order of service	Preservice prayer time extends into the start of service Pastor welcomes people to continue to pray (eight minutes past service start time) Greetings (three minutes of hugging and kissing) Songs of worship led by band (gospel and *coritos*) Scripture reading Sermon Altar call Prayer ministry Announcements Closing prayer (holding hands)	Prelude (two minutes before service) Procession of lights (exact start time) Psalm reading Choral anthem Hymns Greeting Mutual greeting (handshakes for one minute) Prayers Gospel reading Carols Meditation Benediction Postlude

Hopefully everyone will visit worshiping communities from different ethnic and socioeconomic backgrounds so they can experience the joyous discomfort of encountering God in new ways. Christians must practice the discipline of acknowledging differences while suspending judgment. In this chapter I will describe how worship and culture interact. We will explore some models of multiethnic worship and some key contributing components. We will also examine what people have done and are doing, so we can passionately pursue ideas around what could be! What are the possibilities in worship for the increasingly multiethnic millennial church?

WHAT IS MULTIETHNIC WORSHIP?

Over the years it has been my privilege to collaborate with worship leaders who are passionate about creating space for people to practice multiethnic worship. I asked a few of these worship leaders to define multiethnic worship. Allow their words to resonate as we continue exploring worship models and components.

> Multiethnic worship, for me, means worship that acknowledges and honors the diversity of people in God's global and local church, and teaches local congregations to understand and honor that same diversity. This means in a church with more than a single ethnicity the diversity of that church is well represented in the team and song choice; with more than a single language, that each language is represented in the song choice; and that songs from each ethnicity/culture are actually represented in a way that is both honoring to and authentic of the culture they come from. So then the question is, What does "well represented" mean? Simply adding a token member of an ethnicity and allowing them to sing "their song" is not enough. A single

song from another culture is not enough. Throwing in a Spanish-language chorus to a white American song is not enough. Having a special weekend where you do "diverse" songs is not enough. Adding a song from another culture and/or language with no explanation or context is not enough. Rather, multiethnic worship considers songs and narratives from other cultures as integral parts of the planning process, the set lists, the team and its decision making, the stage presence of the team, and the final worship "experience." (Matt Stauffer, Florida)

I believe it starts with a worship team where more than one ethnicity is represented. Not only are they represented, but they take an active role in shaping the worship experience through their cultural experience. This is not only for music but also includes preaching style, calls to worship, benedictions, how Scripture is read, and what languages are represented. Multiethnic worship is more than one differently styled song being added to a homogeneous set of songs. Rather, multiethnic worship is felt within a congregation not as a special moment added to the set but as a part of their overall multiethnic worship culture. (Becky Ykema, Chicago)

An ideal team includes not only members from a variety of ethnic backgrounds but leaders from various ethnic groups. Leadership includes both within the context of congregational worship and within the context of team dynamic. The diversity of the team should reflect the diversity found in the context of the culture. For example, white, black, Latino and Asian in the United States. Where possible, the team makeup should include people from ethnic groups that extend beyond the context of the culture. Instrumentation should be reflective of the instrumentation that is used in the worship expression that is being reflected. Where the instruments are not available, or there is no one who can play the instrument, a synthesizer can be used to recreate a similar sound. While song choice can reflect a particular worship experience, the delivery of the song can vary such that it represents a different worship culture. As mentioned earlier, songs should reflect both the prevailing cultures and extend to the world beyond that context. Shared leadership should include both collaborating on song selection and giving the responsibility entirely to another person. This is only recommended when you have capable leaders to give the responsibility to. Otherwise, it may be helpful to be more involved with the decision. Leadership can be shared within the context of a song or a set. It can also be shared by relinquishing responsibility to another. Vocal leadership should be shared with others when they are adequately skilled to lead successfully. Sharing leadership here includes actively seeking band members' musical ideas. As with other parts of worship, one individual should be the "leader," meaning they have ultimate responsibility for the outcome. This, however, can mean that there is room for collaboration and relinquishing responsibility to others. (Ryan Cook, Texas)

MODELS

In a conversation with my friend Josh, an Asian male, we got onto the topic of models of diverse worship. Since we both were committed to finding authentic cultural expressions and we understood that culture is not static but dynamic, we got onto the topic of fusion music and worship. Both of us had studied jazz in college, so we were well aware of the ways that cultures merge to form beautiful new genres. Music adapts and transforms with time and influences. It seemed whenever we'd select a song, he was prone to select a subgenre within a genre, which was more fusion of two styles than traditional. We went back and forth about how to honor original source traditions that embody the diverse narratives while still innovating in order to stay fresh. It may have seemed that I was not as open to developing new forms, when in reality what I was looking for is balance.

I finally realized how I could explain myself. A restaurant Josh loves serves Korean–Puerto Rican fusion food. Imagine kimchi-covered tostones or a Korean BBQ taco. Yum! I asked him why he enjoyed that food so much. He thought it was the best of both worlds. So, I asked him to imagine that from now on we were only allowed to eat Belly Shack (fusion) and never again allowed to enjoy a bipimbap or bulgogi at San Soo Gab San, or tostones and fried cassava with garlic butter at Senor Pan. "No!" he burst out. "I would definitely want the option of going for Korean BBQ." "Exactly," I said. "New genres of music that are being created are awesome, but they can't replace the good home cooking your mama made for you. It's your go-to comfort food."

Artistic expression is also rooted in some down-home-cooking comfort places that we don't want to throw out. If we are only ever giving people the fusion version, they will miss out on each individual heritage. Heritage connects us not only to musical preferences but to story: the history of our community, the roots of our cultures, the legacy that made us who we are, and how we understand God's story intersecting with ours. Remember, learning one another's God story is what will lead to solidarity in worship.

Four main worship models are widely used in worship that includes multiethnic cultural expressions. These are acknowledgment, blended, fusion and rotation (see table 5.2). There may be variations within each one, but at the core they share commonalities. Let's look at each in more detail.

Table 5.2. Four Models of Multiethnic Worship

Model	Description	Pro	Con
Acknowledgment	A dominant style with a hint of other styles	Simple for experimenting Accessible; only small changes Builds trust with congregations starting or suspicious about multiethnic worship	Cultures on the fringe are not well represented and can even be tokenized Generally only diverse in style, not in other elements or form
Blended	The equal representation of two or more styles	More space for representation, leadership and environment change Utilizes gifted musicians and leaders in communities with multiethnic representation or internationals	Requires musicians that can cross cultures with equal skill Worship whiplash if too many crosscultural moments
Fusion	Mixing styles or creating original music	Music can be developed in multiethnic congregations that are intentionally pursuing reconciliation	Requires gifted musicians and composition Keeps worship focused on musical style, not on elements or form Generally has a dominant style as its foundation
Collaborative Rotation	The leader(s) brings the cultural style and other components of the form	Retains authenticity of original style and form Allows for full empowerment of hosting community in expressing deeper culture's values Congregation can enter more authentically into the experience and story of different communities Proficiency can be achieved among the band	Requires diversity of musicians and leaders who can cross cultures Necessitates the adjustment of not only the music but the whole form of the service Causes confusion for congregants and apprehension about bringing guests

Acknowledgment. The acknowledgment model contains elements of other styles of worship, but the framework is still culturally located in the homogeneous majority expression. The table experience (meal, utensils, music, conversation, drinks, etc.) reflects one dominant culture with a dash of diversity, maybe even a surprise break from the norm. When asked to lead for a women's conference, I was asked to keep the diverse worship to a minimum. The woman proposed that I do three familiar songs and one song from another tradition. She explained that it had been done for the previous conferences, and that was the model they were most comfortable with. She was right about their comfort; a decade later they are still using that model at their conferences. They typically have a diverse team of musicians, and the vocalists are used if their style comes up. The dash of diversity is often one outlier song or prayer for every worship experience. To break it down, there might be one hymn, two contemporary Christian songs and one gospel song.

During these types of services, whether weekly or one-time events, a Latino may be asked to spice up a hymn instrumentally. The deeper cultural values and structure such as time orientation and planning are still white majority. (Or on the flipside, a black congregation might sing a traditional white hymn, but to someone from the German Lutheran church culture it's just not the same.) The overall allotted time for musical worship, sermon and other components typically reflects the majority culture. So, in the context of white dominant, non-charismatic denominations, there will be an average of eighteen minutes of singing (four songs at four to five minutes each), very little instrumental interlude (even if it's written into the chart), call and response, free space for singing or creating melodies or ad-libbing.

Strength. This model allows a congregation to start on a journey. For those who want to experiment it is simple and accessible because it requires small changes. It also can be accomplished without diverse leadership. It's not a full meal, just an appetizer. This is a place to start and build trust with the congregation and leadership. The worship will maintain a core sound and experience that people can expect. They will be stretched, but only for a moment.

Weakness. Churches see this as the goal rather than a step toward deeper solidarity and mutuality. The dominant culture is reflected in the worship, while other cultures are underrepresented and can even be tokenized.

Blended. I see the blended approach most often in churches seeking a more diverse congregation. It mimics the blended style of the worship wars within white evangelical circles. An equal mixture of songs from different cultures is used each Sunday. Imagine a communal meal where each family brings a dish from their own home. The issue here is coordinating the dishes so that people do not get indigestion. Or imagine a progressive dinner, where during a meal everyone moves from home to home and receives a portion of the meal at each place. Of course, the style and flavor depends on each host. So, for example, the worship service includes not just one song in Japanese and the rest traditional hymns, but four countries are represented. Or it may be Wesleyan hymns and two African songs. But the structure, environment and time-oriented nature is from the dominant culture. While there is a desire for the congregation to move into a more inclusive worship practice, the dominant preferences override the ability to move far from the cultural norm. In *The Next Evangelicalism* Soong-Chan Rah describes this type of diversity as a dish made up of all cultures but smothered in ranch dressing:

> With the rejection of the "melting pot" image came the advent of the "salad bowl." In the salad bowl, once again, the wide range of flavors was brought together. But the salad

allowed for each vegetable to retain its flavor. Unfortunately, we often took this rich array of flavors and drenched it in creamy ranch. The dressing overwhelmed and covered all the other vibrant flavors. Even a jalapeno or kimchi covered in creamy ranch would come out tasting like creamy ranch. We may have all the different flavors in once place, but our style of worship, our style of preaching and our approach to community life reflect a form of cultural dressing that covers all of the other flavors and drowns them out.[1]

The use of a smothering dressing does not happen only in Anglo settings; communities of color might use Louisiana Hot Sauce, Tapatio or sriracha.[2]

Strength. Blended worship enables a church to experiment with style, but not form or function. It is accessible to those who want to start being culturally diverse with minimal discomfort. There is more space for representation, leadership and environment change. It utilizes gifted musicians and leaders in communities with multiethnic representation.

Weakness. This style tends to have diversity only within the music. Other elements such as the call to worship, prayer, readings and arts are not diverse. Furthermore, the form of the service is usually driven in a production- and time-oriented fashion, not allowing for the space, mystery or freedom that is at the root of some worship expressions. It requires one set of musicians who can cross cultures with equal skill. Participants can become confused about what is coming next and experience worship whiplash if there is too much variety.

Fusion. The fusion model encourages mixing music styles or even creating original music, thus creating a new sound. The idea stems from the belief in a universal sound that appeals to all people. Israel Houghton's style, considered crosscultural, is seen by some as the universal language of worship. Houghton sings,

It ain't a black thing
it ain't a white thing
it ain't a color thing
it's a kingdom thing.[3]

The new sound has a foundational genre as the base. This kingdom sound is a fusion of gospel and rock, though it's based in gospel vocally and thematically.

Strength. Fusion music is typically composed by a small community of artists shaped by similar influences. Fusion allows for new music to be developed in multiethnic communities that are intentionally pursuing reconciliation. It gives birth to new expressions rooted in the experiences of a younger generation and gives them an opportunity to tell their new story. Because it is more compatible with the music people are hearing outside of church, it allows outsiders to connect more easily with the church.

Weakness. This model requires musicians who are composers. As with the other models, it keeps the focus on the music, not the entire worship experience. This develops a façade that the worship is a new culture altogether, yet the liturgy and practices themselves are rooted in modern concert-and-sermon approaches.[4] Another weakness is that fusion is almost always a minority culture sound that is heavily influenced by dominant culture rock or contemporary music, which raises the question if it is a form of modernization or assimilation.[5] If so, then legacy is absent and the history of a people diluted.

Collaborative rotation. The collaborative rotation model rotates leaders or teams on a weekly or monthly basis, during which there is one dominant worship expression. The services are hosted by leaders from within the culture represented and retain both the style and form of that culture. Imagine a small group taking turns meeting in one another's homes. Each week the host prepares a meal of their choice. During the Christmas season, for example, why not immerse your congregation in an experience of worship through parranda—the Puerto Rican version of Christmas caroling? A small group of friends gathers together to surprise another friend by arriving at his or her home to sing, accompanied by some sort of instrument, either guitarras, tamboriles, güiro or maracas. In a worship setting, leading a religious parranda song for worship would be great, but what about surprising the congregation by having people come up the aisles with percussion, dancing and singing, and inviting others to join in?

Strength. The strength of this model is that it can move people beyond the music to the experience and story of different communities through teaching, prayers, rituals and testimony. Worship retains the authenticity of original style and form. Every community is given an opportunity to lead and fully enter into the form and style of worship within other cultures. Collaborative rotation allows for full empowerment of the hosting community in expressing deeper cultural values. This creates space for shared leadership and mutuality in worship. Proficiency can be achieved through rotating teams, and everyone will learn new styles and expressions.

Weakness. Collaborative rotation is limited by the leadership at hand and their ability to not just mimic music but provide true worship leadership. If musicians are not rotating and they only play within their tradition, they will not be encouraged to stretch beyond their preferences. If musicians are rotating, they may experience fatigue constantly learning new music. This model requires diversity of musicians from different backgrounds. This kind of worship can be seen as a "flavor of the week" approach to worship. And it may be difficult for visitors to grasp the worship style if they only visit once or twice. Congregants, therefore, may be uneasy about bringing visitors.

CAUTIONS

With over a decade of professional research and practice, I have noticed a few things about the various models of multiethnic worship. While varied approaches have been successful in developing multiethnic congregations, leaders should not choose a worship model for pragmatic reasons; attention should be given to *why* we do what we do. As the church is led in worship, they will internalize values based on the model presented. It's all about intentionality! Pastors need to work diligently to develop an overall vision of sets and who is leading and where they are going. Professor Monique Ingalls says,

> Good worship leading is like good writing: from the start, there's a clear sense of the overall objective or purpose, and constant reference is made back to those throughout the set. Some worship leading in evangelical churches today tends toward the "choose-your-own-adventure" variety, eschewing set themes or any overarching direction. This model is often informed by radical individualism, where leaders believe that the Spirit will take worshipers where they need to go if they enter into the experience deeply enough. But while intentions may be good, this refusal to lead often leaves congregation members lost. Worse, it brings feelings of failure or disillusionment to worshipers who, for whatever reason, aren't in a position to chart their own course. There are obvious anthropological and theological problems with this particular practice, but it remains prevalent.[6]

Intentionality about which style to use in worship is often missing. It seems many of us prefer a buffet rather than having a chef prepare a good meal and pair it with a perfect wine. When we have too many styles and too many leaders, we can cause confusion or indigestion.

CURRENT LANDSCAPE

Fascinating research has been done on race in the church. Some books reporting sociological research on multiethnic churches (including *One Body, One Spirit* and *United by Faith*) have included chapters on worship, and a few focus exclusively on worship (such as *Worship Across the Racial Divide*).[7] The dialogue on worship has specifically centered on the role of multicultural worship in developing multiethnic congregations. In earlier writings George Yancey and Mosaic Network found that multicultural worship is one of the top three necessities in developing diverse congregations. Recently Gerardo Marti, department chair of sociology at Davidson College, counters the theory that diverse worship will lead to diverse congregations in his book *Worship Across the Racial Divide*. Marti specifically looked at twelve Protestant churches in Southern California and asked, "How do music and worship 'work' in successfully diverse congregations?"[8] While church leaders are looking for the magic bullet in worship that will lead to diverse congregations, Marti says racial unity can't be accomplished through one distinctive worship style. Worship leaders have focused on the sound of the music, but the practice of being together and interacting in worship across racial differences is most important in developing diverse congregations.[9] Marti states,

> I found that paying attention to sound was far less important than the more challenging attempt to pay attention to the complex of practices of the worshiping community in the production and absorption of music. I focused on the musical styles in church services until I came to a growing recognition of music as a social practice, as occurring in an interactive process, and as creating opportunities for shared identity. . . . Musical practice creates opportunities for formulating particular social bonds that transcend racial differences. . . . It is

not the sound of "music" alone but social context that makes music powerful.[10]

I agree that music is only a small portion of the equation. The idea that worship practice or liturgy (the "work of the people") leads to true unity is insightful. However, though multiethnic worship may not increase the statistical diversity of a congregation, it will communicate its values. Hospitality to and solidarity with people on the margins, and mutuality and connection with the global church are not means to an end but part of the kingdom work of God's people. The sociological studies describe what is, but not necessarily what should or could be. Sociologists make observations about the past and present so that we can imagine the future. They are descriptive, not prescriptive. Without informative observations the assumptions we make are unhelpful in moving forward. Marti and others are charged with the important work of describing what has been, and my passion is to patiently take into account serious issues raised by rigorous research in order to envision what could be.

Let's take a look at an example that Marti observes. He argues that church members "accept" the music of the church they are attending and accommodate themselves to the worship styles. He gives some reasons why this might be and then goes on to argue that the research shows that music is not an important factor in deciding on a church. Congregants attend churches based on friends and family and their involvement in the ministry of the church. Once they are there they take on the "congregational identity" and worship style of the church.[11]

This resonates with my own interviews and congregational visits in multiethnic settings. (Remember, multiethnic means 20 percent or more of the congregation is not from the majority group.) The research is helpful for confirming and explaining.[12] I have repeatedly heard that people stay committed to a church because of its mission or their relationships, but they may also describe how their particular expression of worship is missing. Yet, they tolerate the current worship given their overall values. A church may be successfully multiethnic whether it changes the worship style or not, but the congregants may not feel fully ministered to. These congregants' playlist and the church's are completely different. On their own they pray in their own tongue and listen to podcasts of Christian teaching from their cultural context. They learn from the majority, but no one gets to learn from them. If a congregation wanted to make itself diverse, changing the worship alone would not accomplish that. For example, it is not likely a Latino would choose to join a historically Dutch church merely because they sang a song in Spanish. However, if for whatever reason a Latino chose that church as his or her home, a Spanish song would at least communicate that Latinos are welcome. Leading diverse worship creates a welcoming environment for those who feel marginalized—without the pragmatic goal of being multiethnic. Sadly, some churches still will argue that since diverse worship is not necessary for their already-diverse congregation, there is no reason to have it. Even if the congregants are already in the door and committed, should we not still practice values of hospitality, solidarity and mutuality in worship? Should a portion of our church be relegated to an experience of assimilation into our congregational identity and worship style because they are willing to "accept" it?

THREE GUIDING PRINCIPLES

Regardless of which model is favored, three principles should guide a church that wants its worship to be inclusive.

Diverse music. Music is not everything. In fact, it is only part of the worship equation, but it is an important part. The arts are rooted in the experience of a community; they tell a story. They are written out of an encounter with God, his Word and one's personal life; they reflect a theology that has been developed. When I speak of music I am referring to three aspects: lyrics, melody and instrumentation. Multiethnic worship, at its basic level, should have diverse cultural expressions of song, dance, arts, poetry, language and instrumentation. When adopting these cultural elements into liturgical practices, though, it's important to navigate the difference between a stereotype and an archetype. In the *Inclusion Paradox* Andrés Tapia states, "An archetype is the tendency of a group of people to behave in a certain way. A stereotype is the belief that all members of a cultural group behave according to the archetype for that group."[13] Not all Latinos sing in Spanish. Not all black people like gospel. Not all white people sing hymns or play guitar. Not all hipsters play mandolin. To say these are always present is to stereotype. To say there is no consistent presence of these elements is foolish. To have diverse worship you must consider the breadth of ethnic expressions. I encourage you to access the many resources that are available regarding different worship cultures. Some books, websites and articles can be found in appendix B. Appendix I also includes summary descriptions of four major North American ethnic categories of worship.

Diverse platform. One white male once told me he attended a black church for over a year and never considered joining the choir. He confessed that not seeing white people on the platform caused him to internalize the message that he was there as an observer. It's shallow if people aren't invited to collaborate, and conversely powerful when people see themselves in leadership. Inclusion is not helpful if it's mere representation, tokenism, but when space is provided to work across differences it is empowering. Tokenism pats itself on the back for having an Asian person on the worship team. Empowerment allows space for that Asian person to influence what happens on the team and on Sunday morning.

Diverse leadership. A diverse group of leaders that are culturally competent is key to multicultural worship; this type of collaborating community encourages the development of a robust theology of and approaches to worship. Such collaboration allows worship leaders to include their traditions in a way that someone from the outside can't. The depth of collaboration will depend on the model. A shared leadership model (see chap. 4) views inclusion as central to the team's philosophy and practice of multiethnic worship. Note, though, that the more diverse, not only racially but culturally and socio-economically, the more the team's assumptions will be challenged.

The application of these three principles may vary depending on context. Churches with long-standing traditions (e.g., mainline and Catholic) may have more incentive to remain with the lectionary or hymns since tradition and conformity with the church across the globe are highly valued. However, it must be noted that aside from pieces dating back to the early church, much of the liturgy is shaped by and rooted in Western culture. Let's examine one case study as an example of how to mitigate these issues. Katelin Hansen is the director of music at the United Methodist Church for All People (4AllPeople.org), a multirace, multiclass church in Columbus, Ohio. She describes her worship team, music and approach this way:

> We have two teams of leaders that alternate each week. Both teams have two white (including myself) and two black singers. We also have subs who are from a range of other backgrounds, though these demographics are not as prominent in our neighborhood. The instrumentalists are the same each week and include a keyboard, guitar (switches between electric and acoustic), bass, drum set, congas and other percussion. We incorporate a range of styles along the way, including black gospel, hymns, CCM, multilingual songs and Appalachian music.[14] Ideally, each service touches each one

of these genres. The pastor likes theme-driven services, so some days the theme fits one culture's theological priorities more than another, and that's okay too.

We follow a structured service outline every week: an intro, a call to worship, two community songs, community prayer time, a prayer song, an offertory song/special music, announcements, Scripture reading, sermon and closing song. Although I grew up in a format that consisted of thirty minutes of music followed by the sermon, the liturgical format of our current worship service results in several breaks between songs. I am mindful of the issue of musical flow and try to weave the community songs together despite there being breaks between them. I try to bridge them thematically, rhythmically or just connect them through words of prayer.

Beyond the music we're intentional about the images on our PowerPoints, the art around the sanctuary, as well as who serves as Scripture readers, and ushers, etc. For lay committees and new hires we are also very aware of the church demographics, which largely match our neighborhood (50 percent black, 42 percent white, 4 percent Latino). We also regularly verbalize our values and our goals to the congregation from the pulpit, from the song leadership.[15]

Katelin's context is interesting in that she works within a denominational tradition that is more "high church" and yet is able to create spaces of worship that reflect people of different backgrounds within this more traditional structure. It reminds me of an invitation I received to plan an intentionally diverse worship service for an Anglican church. Most of the diverse worship I had seen had been in the context of evangelical free churches or nondenominational churches that were not connected to any substantial liturgical history, so this intrigued me.

The church congregants were primarily wealthy people and seminary students from the suburbs. However, they communicated a desire to become more hospitable to the working-class Hispanic residents in the area. The service followed a traditional formal liturgy and lasted approximately an hour and a half. For those who have never visited an Anglican service, it begins with a call to worship, moves to the Word and climaxes with the Eucharist. Services end with a benediction and sending forth. We did not make dramatic changes to the service structure or format but added elements. We chose to pass the peace, saying "La paz de Cristo esté contigo. Y con tu espiritu" because it is a familiar act and accessible phrase. The meaning is significant and would not get lost.

Since the Eucharist is the pinnacle of the Anglican service, it is extremely important to create enough space for people to reflect on what we are celebrating. The song "Mighty to Save" tells the gospel story and proclaims that we only boast in Jesus and his work. It also declares that he has paid our ransom on the cross. We are proclaiming and apprehending that Jesus is mighty to save. Since it is an easy chorus, moving from English to Spanish is easy and can be repeated as needed, and the message will be cemented in the minds and hearts of the congregants. It also celebrates Jesus' resurrection power. I wanted to make sure the tone of the table would not be one of sorrow, which is heavily emphasized in Western expressions of the cross, but thanksgiving, a common emphasis in Latino cross theology. The last upbeat song allowed us to end in celebration as we shared in remembering Christ's work in our lives and his future return.

In this setting, where the overall structure is already set, inclusion of diverse songs and elements within that order seemed most appropriate. There is opportunity for creativity within liturgical elements in light of cultural differences, which in this case would extend hospitality to Hispanic residents. Perhaps the amount of time and intensity given for celebration could change. More horizontal dimensions in worship, that is, more congregation-congregation response and less leader-congregation response, could be included. The amount of change to the liturgy would depend on the stage of change the congregation is in and on the church leadership.

Be creative. What Katelin is doing in the context of the United Methodist tradition is creative. I was impressed by her ability to apply the principles of diverse music, platform and leadership within her tradition. It reminded me that there is indeed no recipe for perfect multiethnic worship. There are only communities of people learning from trial and error how to provide atmospheres of worship that communicate "We welcome you"; "We stand with you"; "We need you."

KEY CONCEPTS

- There are many forms of multiethnic worship, each with its benefits and gaps.

- Diverse music, platform and leadership are crucial to every journey of healthy multiethnic worship.

- Diverse worship should not be a tool for growth but an expression of hospitality, solidarity and mutuality in reconciliation.

FOR REFLECTION

- What is multiethnic worship?

- Which models of diverse worship have you seen in practice? Why do you think those models were used?

- How have you practiced or seen practiced diverse platform, diverse music and diverse leadership?

FOR DISCUSSION

- How does our community do multiethnic worship? Where are we on the spectrum?

- What is driving why we do diverse worship?

- How can we structure our services to include diversity in our music, platform and leadership?

Prayer: Lord, help us to not look for easy answers or models to mimic, but give us the courage to consider how we are allowing ourselves to be exposed to and molded by new experiences with your people.

IT'S NOT JUST THE FOOD

Components of
Diverse Worship

was invited to the home of one of my Korean American student leaders. Her father was a pastor of a local church, and I was interested in meeting her family as a way of growing in my mentorship of her. I had Korean friends as a child and had Korean peers in ministry, but I had not been a minister visiting a Korean pastor's home. I emailed and called a handful of my friends and asked them what I should bring. I knew it was fruit, but what kind? When I arrived at the home with Asian pears and Concord grapes, the student smiled at me, pleased I had brought the appropriate gifts for his community. Obviously, the fruit was to eat, but it was also a symbol. My friends helped me visit well. Another time, when gathering with some Indian friends, I observed that each time I finished my plate the food kept coming. I would eat the last bite, express how good it was and immediately a spoonful would hit my plate again. I was going to burst because I did not know what I was communicating. I later learned that I needed to leave some uneaten food on my plate to communicate I was done.

As a Latina working in a non-Latino context, I've had to learn new symbols and the meanings behind them. I've had to learn that different tables have different meanings.

There is much more to a table gathering than food. Don't get me wrong, it matters to me what someone is going to serve. However, it's not the only factor. When invited to an event, our questions move beyond the food to include table etiquette. Is the dress code casual or formal? Are we expected to bring something to contribute? Or will bringing something offend the host? When we arrive, who do we address first? Should we greet them with a kiss, take a bow or shake hands? Do we take off our shoes when we walk into the home? Is there talking at the table? Is there music? Who do we compliment for the food? Can we add seasoning to the dishes served? Do we retire to the living room or stay at the table? These never-ending questions can be overwhelming, but all are components of a table gathering. Coming to the table is not just about the food!

Many worship leaders focus exclusively on the music and not on other aspects of the service, including Scripture reading, prayers, arts, the Lord's Supper or the sermon. This may be due to the way free churches plan services. As with the table, when it comes to worship we must think beyond the songs (food). If we want to create spaces where people from every nation, tribe, tongue and class feel welcomed, we too must look at symbols and meaning. In this chapter I will help us examine the components of multiethnic worship. We will move beyond an iTunes genre to consider culture and context, developing cultural intelligence necessary for the multiethnic future of the church.

Russell Yee, author of *Worship on the Way*, says,

[All churches] are shaped by cultural matters of language, music, time, schedule, posture, gesture, movement, deportment, gender, generation, architecture, decoration, furniture, technology, dress, and leadership. Why does your church's music use a twelve-tone equal temperament scale based on an A = 440 Hz tuning? Why do church buildings in your neighborhood have crosses as architectural features? Why does the person up front speaking in your worship service generally stand up while everyone else sits down? These are all matters of culture. And these are all matters that Scripture largely leaves up to us. There is not one complete worship service even *described* in any detail in the New Testament, let alone *prescribed*.[1]

KISS, BOW OR SHAKE HANDS: READING AND CREATING AN ENVIRONMENT

As a business student I was asked to read the book *Kiss, Bow, or Shake Hands* in our international business class. The professor wanted his future entrepreneurs to possess intercultural competence. How are business meetings handled in Spain or Kazakhstan? When do Chinese believe it's appropriate to discuss finances? In order to be effective in reaching our audience we needed to know how to communicate well. Likewise, good worship theory and practice keep in mind contextualization and crosscultural competency. How do we creatively plan the elements necessary for a multiethnic worship experience? What works in this particular context?

The discipline of anthropology, mainly cultural anthropology, which studies humans and their cultures, can and should be applied to the ministry of music and arts in worship. This discipline allows us to see how a community practices worship. I explain this in *The Mission of Worship*:

Each culture focuses on an attribute of God's character that comes out of the lived experience of that community. Various themes of spirituality are magnified through our particular ethnic lenses. Here are some of Chandler's specific observations on how cultural perspectives highlight particular aspects of God's identity or experiences with God:

- Latin American worship is about celebrating life no matter what the circumstances. It is a lively worship that brings them to trust God in the present as a community. They identify with Scriptures like Ecclesiastes that call us to laughter and joy alongside crying and grief.

- For African Christians there is a strong sense of God's power to bring freedom. The gospel is one of freedom that releases us to worship with victory.

- East Asian Christians exalt a God who is bigger than we can imagine. Worship, therefore, is about unboxing God so we can see him in his glory.

- Eastern European worship reveals a majestic and holy God.

- South Asians see God as a teacher who models and walks with us.

- For Middle Eastern Christians a life of worship is about perseverance and running the race (Hebrews 12:2).[2]

Knowing the theme and essence (or purpose) of worship in a community helps ensure that the themes and values, which go beyond instrumentation and musical style, are being represented—like an iceberg, which has 90 percent of its mass beneath the surface.[3] Once we have our context in mind and our team (with some form of shared leadership) in place, we want to clarify which of the four models of diverse worship (acknowledgment, blended, fusion, rotation) we are committed to and why.

Let's consider two distinct contexts.

Church of the Nations is an international community of people in the Minneapolis area that has decided to make their worship intentionally inclusive. Given their international makeup, they use global worship music mostly composed of folk songs and traditional hymns from the major cultures and the most commonly spoken languages represented in the church and surrounding community. They are still considering how global cosmopolitan music can be brought in for the younger generation. They are a multicongregational church that skips individual weekly services once a month for a joint worship service and fellowship dinner. They have considered three different approaches for these monthly gatherings. Table 6.1 outlines the pros and cons of each.

Table 6.1. Potential Church of the Nations Monthly Gatherings

Congregations Rotating	Multicongregational	Multicultural
Each congregation takes a service and leads the others in worship (maybe twice a year there is a joint team).	Leaders from one cultural expression rotate, but the team is made up of all congregations.	Leaders from various cultural expressions rotate, and the team is made up of all congregations.
Music and liturgy from the leading community are used.	Music and liturgy from the leader's community are used.	Music and liturgy from all communities are used.
Teams only lead worship from their own ethnicity.	Team members from all ethnicities lead in one another's styles.	Team members from all ethnicities lead in one another's styles.
It produces cultural immersion with an opportunity to affect the aesthetic space, Lord's Supper, forms of prayer and time orientation.	It produces cultural immersion with an opportunity to affect the aesthetic space, Lord's Supper, forms of prayer and time orientation.	A new culture is created.
English and the leader's language are used.	English and the leader's language are used.	All languages are used.

City Church is a community in New York City area of second-generation millennials from different ethnic communities, the majority of which are white, Asian and black. They are located in a predominantly Latino community. Most people from each ethnic community have a strong connection to their respective heritage. There is not much of an international presence. Since they are located in an urban center, they have decided to pursue models of multiethnic worship. They have considered three different approaches. Table 6.2 outlines the pros and cons of each.

Table 6.2. Potential City Church Monthly Gatherings

Cultural Immersion	Multicultural	Third Culture
Worship rotates between different styles and forms—much like churches that have a traditional service and contemporary service, except all people experience both. (Imagine hymns and liturgical readings one week and contemporary Christian music, ad-libbed prayers and a sermon the next.)	The worship team uses all styles and forms within one service—much like a blended service. (Imagine hymns with an organ and a full worship rock band in the same service.)	A team is made up of different ethnicities and the community attempts to blend the expressions into a new fusion expression. (Imagine a hymn rearranged with full band.)
The elements and timing of each element change from week to week.	The elements and timing could change from week to week but are likely rooted in the cultural expression of the majority tradition.	A new doxology arises that may be informed by different elements, but does not likely resemble any of the original elements.

GATHERING THE RIGHT INGREDIENTS

Worship planning already starts when the team commits to the guiding principles of hospitality, solidarity and mutuality at the table. They continue planning by selecting the overall approach to shared leadership and a model of worship. These serve as the foundation for selection of songs, liturgical elements and other details. In his famous book *Worship Old and New*, theologian Robert Webber states that we ought to consider three levels of conversation regarding worship: content, structure and style. Under the topic of structure, Webber suggests four components of worship that should be in every worship service: Gathering, Word, Supper and Sending.[4] In the article "Robert E. Webber's Legacy: Ancient

Future Faith and Worship," Joan Huyser-Honig, freelance writer with Calvin Institute of Christian Worship, points out that Webber would often remind people how hosting guests for a meal is a lot like worship. Both meals and worship require a spirit of hospitality and follow a fourfold pattern.

Gathering: You warmly welcome people at the door.

Word: You engage deep conversation at home and a sermon at church.

Table: You share a meal.

Sending: You part with hugs at home and a benediction in church.[5]

Worship leaders and committees develop song lists consistent with the values of the community. Then the worship leaders give guidance and shepherd the time accordingly. When worshiping with an international gathering, the components (songs, speakers, prayers, languages) of the service should reflect this global community. Songs in multiple languages and testimonies from different countries make sense.[6] The age demographic will influence whether they use folk songs in indigenous styles or more contemporary music that is still global. I have seen generational differences arise. Older forms of global worship (folk), developed by the previous generation of ethnodoxologists, work in more tribal contexts. But with a gathering of urban youth who are praying for and are being mobilized to speak to the violence in their city, more modern urban expressions of worship are appropriate.[7] The components might be spoken word, dance and songs in musical styles such as hip-hop, reggae and reggaetón. Maybe the gathering is denominational and is rooted in a more traditional liturgy (e.g., Swedish or Dutch expressions). We need to consider whether we are creating a space for the traditional folks, the younger leaders or those who feel marginalized just by being there. Or do we creatively craft for all?

The following are things to consider when selecting songs:

1. Song selection criteria. Choose criteria that will allow you to select songs that make sense for your community. For example:

- Choose songs that work for your context. Who is represented in your community (generation, ethnicity, etc.)?

- Choose songs that speak to the backgrounds of different people. In your congregation you may have people who have suffered not only personally but collectively due to systemic injustices.

- Choose songs that reflect those in your community you wish to reach through hospitality (a racial group, subculture, etc.).

- Choose songs that are theocentric and teach good theology. Many argue that hymns are the best due to their thoroughness, but word count and depth are not necessarily correlated. There are many African American spirituals that repeat the same words but are robust in properly framing God's character.

- Choose songs meant to be sung in community for congregational worship. Other music should be used as special arts.

- Choose songs that speak to God and to one another about God.

- Choose a variety of song themes (celebration, confession, lament, praise, mission, devotion, adoration, submission, surrender).

- Choose songs (and keys) that are melodically simple and singable, keeping gender and range in mind.

- Choose songs from diverse traditions and with diversity in those traditions.[8]

- Choose songs that are connected to your themes and mission.

2. Song research. The following are some tools to use when searching for appropriate music.

- Search the web. (For CCM go to familiar websites that allow you to search for most current songs. A few are planningcenteronline. com, CCLI.com, iTunes [Top Christian and Gospel] and

YouTube videos. If your church uses Planning Center, you can see the top songs used by other churches that use Planning Center.)

- Connect with your denominational resources to see if they have songbooks.

- Interview and learn from worship leaders from different ethnic and socioeconomic backgrounds. Consider what networks you already have.

- Review the list of worship movements and worship artists in appendix C. Look up artists by name on iTunes and YouTube to see which songs are most popular.

3. Song selection process. To help you choose songs, the following ideas are helpful.

- Evaluate the worship songs you've used over the years, talk with others about what has been well-received and make goals for the future.

- Involve voices from the different ethnic communities to influence your worship culture.

- Survey communities with which you have access to gauge the popularity of certain songs. I've developed online surveys to send to friends and surveyed students at conferences and retreats.

- Involve the entire team in the process of selecting songs. While each worship director may do the final selection differently, the team members should give voice from their communities.

- Choose thirty to fifty songs for the year, with less than half being new, to present to the elders, pastoral staff or worship committee.

- Dialogue with folks outside of your usual network on global resources.

- Choose songs for your context: team members, mission and vision, community and so forth.

- Create mashups between songs or fusion arrangements that each offer something beautiful (old and new, different styles, etc.).[9]

- Allow your team to create new arrangements and songs.

- Work with firsthand global resources to help choose and learn songs.

- Test songs along the way to see how people responded to them.

4. Song selection challenges and obstacles. As you choose songs, be aware of the following challenges and obstacles.

- People have strong opinions about worship music. Different camps are critiquing one another, so it is important to have a strong philosophy.

- Learn how to navigate opinions on traditional and contemporary worship within each style.

- Some team members may be unaware of their individual or cultural preferences in song selection.

- Steer clear of prioritizing songs based on being cool or sounding good.

- The worship director must be ready to navigate critical conversations due to strong opinions.

- Some ethnic communities do not have dialogue about worship, which can make it difficult to ask someone to pave the way.

Melissa Vallejo, worship leader and songwriter, was preparing to lead worship for a multinational event.[10] Because of the complexity of leading worship for a gathering consisting of people from dozens of nations, she had over a year to plan. From the coordinators of the event she was given the overall history and purpose of congregational worship at the event. She gathered some information about which primary languages would be used by the speakers, artist and attendees. The people involved in the planning of and speaking at the event gathered for a series of meetings. Melissa was able to build relationships, gather information and develop some ideas about what songs would be helpful at the event. To do this she sought out leaders to ask questions about popular songs in their region of the world. She collected past song lists that had been used at world and regional events. The musical director and a small group of leaders on her team was involved in giving input on songs, including someone from the host country. They circulated a package of thirty songs (see appendix F) that fit the following criteria. The songs should be

1. Congregational. They are for groups to sing.

2. Theocentric. Their focus is exalting God for who he is and our response to him.

3. Melodically simple and singable. This is *very* important! Songs that have repeated words are helpful.

4. Multiethnic/diverse/global worship. The songs are primarily in English, French and Spanish, with some African languages.

5. Anchored in Scripture and mission themes.

6. Hymns known by many in the organization.

Melissa had led crosscultural worship in multiethnic settings before, but this task of working across the globe required using the same tools in a different context. The process required collaboration and empowerment, and helped narrow down hundreds of song options to a manageable amount.

It is very appropriate, and very time consuming, to devote so much to song selection because it's a large part of worship. As we've seen, though, there are many other cultural elements to consider when leading diverse worship. We will examine these more closely in the remaining sections of this chapter.

LITURGICAL ELEMENTS AND FORM

While not all worship traditions speak in terms of liturgy, all include some form of repeated structure, whether formal or informal. The following will help you to think through the liturgical elements of worship.

- Consider the elements from your faith tradition or denomination that are central (frequency of the Lord's Supper, use of the liturgical calendar and lectionary, altar calls, prayer ministry, healing prayer, songbook or worship manual, etc.).

- Consider the expectations of intergenerational and churchwide participation (the role of deacons and elders, and youth and children involvement).

- Think through the components of a service. How might you bring in cultural distinctives within the following components: call to worship, greeting, prayers, passing of the peace, Scripture reading, sermon, prayers of the people, offering, Communion, thanksgiving, blessing, and benediction.[11] How much time will be given to each?

- Consider the role of the arts, including music, dance, visuals and spoken word.

- Consider themes that would apply to people in different stages of life and socioeconomic experiences.

- Visit the Calvin Institute of Christian Worship (worship.calvin .edu) for global liturgical resources.

Excursus: When it becomes about the song. Mark Charles, a Navajo resource development specialist for indigenous worship, says that many approaches to multicultural worship boil down to assimilation. This happens when we take songs from different styles and pack them into the seventy-five-minute (or less) worship service. He explains that because the underlying value of the United States is assimilation, the church has adopted North American cultural perspectives on time perception. Mark explains that this is critically important when considering Navajo worship in a multicultural context. He explains,

> Many times when people talk about contextualizing worship they think about what instruments are we going to use or some type of style. But how do we need to change the structure of our church so that the structure itself communicates that we think this event is sacred? Many of the songs that we sing [in Navajo culture] are longer than most Christian church services. They can easily go on for an hour or two hours, all night long if they have to. The perception of time is different, so the first missionaries thought, *These Navajos don't love God; they are always late for church.* The Navajos thought, *These missionaries don't love God; look how short their service is.* Two completely different ways to understand the world.[12]

Just when Navajo people are beginning to relate to God and to one another, the service ends. Thus the interaction is not completed, which is not sacred or holy or respecting God in a Navajo culture. Table 6.3 explores a few concepts between these two views of time.[13]

A church in Denver hosted a Navajo worship service about once a month. It included cooking, singing, sharing needs and concerns, retelling parables, feasting (fry bread, mutton, stew) and Communion with tortillas. The service lasted from about 2 p.m. to 10 p.m. This wonderful service valued the Navajo people and was the appropriate place for them to offer their traditional songs. If these songs were sung in the context of a Western service, they would be appreciated, but we would not get the whole experience, which includes a huge meal and no time constraints. It simply doesn't work. Mark argues, "It should be expressed in the way and place it was supposed to be expressed."[14]

Table 6.3. Western and Navajo Perceptions of Time

Western Perception of Time	Navajo Perception of Time
Linear	Circular
Once an event is in the past, it is complete and cannot be revisited.	If an event is in the past or was missed, there is not as much reason for concern. The event usually comes around again.
Life is organized by creating a schedule.	Life is organized by completing tasks or events.
Value and importance are communicated by keeping and honoring the schedule.	Value and importance are communicated not by starting and arriving on time, but by staying until the interaction is over or the task is complete.
Example: If I make plans to meet someone for lunch at noon and do not show up until 1 p.m., I owe that person an apology because my tardiness is offensive. I did not honor our schedule and did not value his or her time.	Example: If I make plans to meet someone on the reservation at noon and do not show up until 1 p.m., there is usually no need for me to apologize. But once we are talking, if I am constantly looking at my watch or I suddenly announce that I need to leave, I have committed an offense. I did not allow the interaction to come to its natural completion.

SERVICE PLANNING

It is critically important to note that form is as meaningful as style. This is why I said earlier that one of the models of diverse worship changes the style of the elements but prefers the form of the dominant group. Song selection, team and liturgical elements are significant to both style and form. When I use the word *form*, I mean "order or structure of worship." Every community has liturgy whether they are aware of it or not. This normal pattern can be explicit or implicit, but everyone has one. John Witvliet states,

Form reveals what's most important to a congregation (usually what a congregation considers to be most sacramental). Form implies an understanding of worship. Form or pattern is not just about convenience or efficiency. It's deeply theological. It portrays and reflects a community's understanding of who God is and how God is approached.[15]

He gives the following examples of what is the most important service element in different denominational traditions:

- Anglican Mass   Eucharist
- Presbyterian worship service   sermon
- Baptist revival service   altar call
- Charismatic worship service   music

A community's understanding and life with God shapes the form of worship. This is why, for example, many white evangelical churches pay the most attention to the preparation, placement and time allotment of the sermon. Even the musical worship is only to set up and respond to the sermon. Worship in itself is not seen as a ministry of the Word, where one can learn about God. Pastors and church leaders must become aware of what they are communicating theologically by the form of their service. In service planning for multiethnic worship, we must consider which of these forms must be altered to embrace the breadth of emphases of an increasingly diverse community.

Many people ask me how much diversity is too much or how I handle learning fatigue and how to appropriately stretch the community. A group of worship leaders who implement different approaches to multiethnic worship were asked what they suggested to avoid worship whiplash.[16] They responded,

> I normally only utilize three genres of music; more is too whiplashy. Even in homogeneous worship it's normal to move between two or three styles of music (slow, fast, contemplative, praise, etc.), so using those transitions to also transition genres commonly eases the pain of the transition. Also, using teaching transitions (e.g., "This is a new song," "This is a diff language," etc.) is a helpful way to reduce the whiplash

that happens when you transition genres directly with no warning. (Matt Stauffer, Florida)

I personally wouldn't mix more than two genres in a single worship service. This gives enough space to honor the genres being represented. In particular, I wouldn't include more than two because creating a particular worship experience extends beyond song choice. If you only create space for a song, you may not be able to adequately reflect the experience of worshiping in a particular culture. In instances where multiple genres are being represented, I would consider it the worship leader's responsibility to address this through the way they pastor congregants in worship. They should give clear explanations about what is happening and how congregants can be engaged. (Ryan Cook, Texas)

How many genres in one service depends on what is called for within the service and also what our diverse teams can execute given their skill level. On average we usually get at least two different styles. For coping with worship whiplash, transitions are key. Making sure that the genres work with one another and also being creative and thoughtful about arrangements and not just doing a genre for its sake, but for the feeling, thought and atmosphere we are trying to create for worship. (Nakhia Grays, Baltimore)

While there are so many forms to consider, let's take only one variable and work with it: children! What do you do with children in your service? Do they sit with their parents or together? Is there a children's sermon? Are the children dropped off at kids' church before worship, or do they march out at some point during the service? What happens when children cry or speak during service? Are parents supposed to shush them?[17] What does the preacher do to include those who are too old for kids' church but too young to appreciate a sermon on justification?

There is so much to consider! The kids are just one example. Even if the only thing churches consider is the music, let's not be too hard on them. It can be overwhelming to think about the dozens of aspects of planning influenced by culture. If only 17 percent of all churches in the United States are multiethnic and only a small portion of those intentionally pursue diverse forms of worship, that means doing something is better than doing nothing at all.

Planning steps. If you are willing to take some risk and are moving in the direction of pursuing intentional multiethnic worship, the following steps will help you to implement it.

1. Gather a community of people to plan (pastors, staff, worship team, worship committee). Train your team with a focus on learning about multiethnic worship through annual planning retreats, monthly discussions and attending worship conferences.

2. Have the group work on a vision and plan to move people forward in understanding and participating in multiethnic worship. Make decisions about organization, form and style. It is important to know what current traditions are nonnegotiable.

3. Assess the gifts and resources in your church. Select people to arrange music, create Sunday experiences and manage logistics. It is important to know what you need and who can do it.

4. Once you are committed to some model of diverse worship, consider what styles and languages should be used in your service. Regardless of your model, I suggest not mixing more than two styles on a Sunday if you want time to deeply enter into the essence of that expression of worship. For example, in the African American tradition a song starts the worship time, but it's only a springboard into moments of prayer, exhortation,

ad-libbed songs or space to be in God's presence. One gospel song is not adequate.

5. Develop a functioning worship template that can be altered to reflect the essence and emphasis of the ethnic communities in your church. (Remember that form can change depending on value. A friend of mine always says, "It's not really black church until you sing about the blood for twenty minutes." That means, of course, that eighteen minutes for the entire musical worship set will not suffice!)

6. Making changes step by step.

   - Start with a themed Sunday (e.g., Mission Sunday, MLK Sunday, Latino Heritage Sunday).

   - Introduce a song or prayer from a different community, or develop multiple elements that Sunday. People are more open on special Sundays.

   - Use your normal form, but alter the language or style (e.g., read psalms in three different languages; have the choir do a gospel spiritual).

   - Invite a guest leader to lead in his or her community's style. Congregations are usually more open to guests.

   - Choose two to four songs and introduce them into the normal form of worship on a random Sunday. This will signal that multiethnic worship is not only for special Sundays.

   - Make sure your introductions are pastoral and clear: "This morning we are going to worship in solidarity with . . ." not just "Now it's time to sing in Spanish." People need to be guided.

Questions around song selection, liturgical elements and form can be overwhelming, but all are important components of a table gathering. Coming to the table is not just about the food! The people in your congregation, current and new, will be blessed by all the thought, prayer and planning invested in your congregational gatherings.

Dr. Robin Harris, director of the Center for Excellence in World Arts at Graduate Institute of Applied Linguistics, and Josh Davis, director of Proskuneo School of the Arts (proskuneo.org), crafted a worship service titled "'Blessed Are the Persecuted': Worshiping in Solidarity with the Persecuted Church." They gathered a community to share leadership and together (often by email) committed to a model of blended worship, developed a vision around the overall biblical theme, researched the places affected by persecution and considered the songs they could learn. Rooted in the Beatitudes, this service used multiple leaders, global songs from the countries experiencing persecution and responsive reading of Scriptures and written prayers. The result was a well-crafted experience for people to enter into solidarity with the global church.[18] This service as well as others in this chapter can be found in appendix D.

KEY CONCEPTS

- Multiethnic worship is not merely about music but includes form and liturgy.

- You can't do it on your own. Invite people to come alongside you in your journey.

- Diverse worship requires much intentionality. When crafting multiethnic worship services, it is necessary to answer who, what, when, where, how and why.

FOR REFLECTION

- Planning and leading multiethnic worship can be overwhelming. What are some steps you can take as you look to grow in preparing multiethnic worship services?

- Who do you need with you as you take this worship journey? Which friends from different backgrounds—pastors, musicians or ministers—do you need to learn from?

- Make a list of words that describe worship in your current community. What are some of the theological values present?

FOR DISCUSSION

- List the elements (liturgy) of your worship service, including variants for special events (e.g., Easter week). Why are these present? (You may need to consult with older members or leaders in the congregation.)

- Discuss with people from different worship backgrounds how you could adjust aspects of service to enjoy worship from their culture. How should this be done? Who should participate?

- Take a look at tables 6.1 and 6.2 and list with your team what you observe.

Prayer: Lord, fill me with excitement, creativity and wisdom as I envision multiethnic worship. Give me insight and self-awareness to evaluate well, and humility to let go of preferences that create barriers.

seven

GUESS WHO'S COMING TO DINNER

Creating Culture Change

A large church in a major city was on a journey of multiethnic worship. The suburban church had historically been a few thousand white folks from upper-middle-class backgrounds. There were seasons in which the church grew in diversity. The worship director had a particular passion to grow the congregation in diverse worship, so he began to experiment by bringing in people to lead worship with him for special occasions that warranted a more global/diverse feel. After a few years of exposing his church, he hired a diverse team of artists who could help him create art that was more inclusive of other cultures. The church began to expand its gospel choir and musicians to duplicate other styles (particularly gospel). He began to use others to lead songs during the services. The church continued to grow in exposure over a five-year period.

One day it came to the attention of the staff that the worship was not connecting with some members of the congregation, primarily because they had no idea what to expect week to week. They were not sure who would be leading or what style was going to be used. It became increasingly difficult for them to feel safe inviting their friends to church. As a result the leadership decided to discontinue the use of multiethnic songs and diverse leadership. They stopped using as much formal liturgy, gospel or global worship. They reverted back to the use of only CCM. Although they occasionally used fusion gospel, it was executed in the style of rock. The worship leaders became background vocalists, and many of them left the ministry. By the end of the transition, all that remained was a core band with a lead vocalist and a couple of background vocalists. Retreating to the original monocultural style of worship encouraged people to once again invite their friends. The *intentional* decision to value safety for majority culture people interested in inviting friends had an adverse affect on the diversity of the worship even though the congregation was still multicultural:

This scenario raises important questions:

- What did they mean when they said they did not feel "safe" inviting their friends?

- What else could have been done in order to avoid completely eliminating diverse expressions of worship music?

- What questions could have been posed to the worship leaders and staff to clarify the situation?

- What did the decision communicate to the congregation? To people of color?

- How might the worship leaders have been affected by this decision?

The core issue was discomfort by some of the congregants whose voices mattered more to the church. I was not surprised when I heard the end of the story. From the start I didn't think the model being used was sustainable.

Mark Charles, worship consultant to the Christian Reformed Church, wrote about his own discomfort in worship. He helpfully said,

> It is about embracing the discomfort of disunity. You can study and learn about a culture as an outsider or even as an observer. But you cannot worship that way. Worship is personal and intimate. I would love to say that with all of my travels and the many peoples, cultures and languages I have worshipped with, that I no longer feel awkward when I encounter something new. But that is not true and if I am completely honest I have to say "I felt uncomfortable."[1]

We must be skilled at developing processes of change that help people embrace the discomfort.

The iconic 1960s movie *Guess Who's Coming to Dinner*, remade in 2005 as *Guess Who?*, brings clear images of a family that was unwilling to allow the "other" to the table. The tension of the movie is heightened by the prospect of an interracial relationship. The discomfort increases when it is not merely about inviting another over for a meal but rather making a covenant commitment with someone from a different ethnic or racial background. The original movie was more intense than the remake, which poked fun at the intolerance of the black father (portrayed by Bernie Mac). The families were faced with the reality that by including the "other" things would change. It would no longer be business as usual to those inside the family.

The same goes for churches that desire to embrace people of every ethnicity, culture and class. They have the responsibility to help their congregation wake up to the reality that the good old days are not going to continue; brighter days are around the corner.

Depending on the congregation, this ignites many fears. For intergenerational churches the fear is that the newer generation is trying to replace the old. "Out with the old; in with the new" is an

American motto that places higher value on fresh perspectives. It's understandable, therefore, that older people feel they are becoming obsolete. Older church leaders may be asking themselves if they have anything of value to offer. Is newer always better? These fears are real and should be treated with care when pursuing change.

In "Here We Are to Worship: Six Principles That Might Bring a Truce to the Age-Old Tension Between Tradition and Popular Culture," theologians Brad Harper and Paul Louis Metzger affirm the need for retaining both:

> So what is the solution to the worship wars, to the battle over contemporary versus traditional worship forms? ... [T]he answer must lie in a dialectical, yes-and-no approach. When contemporary forms draw a broad community of worshipers more effectively into authentic engagement with the Trinitarian God, yes. When they accurately represent the biblical gospel, yes. When contemporary forms present an image of God or the gospel that lacks the fullness of or distorts the image given by historic Christian tradition and the biblical narrative, no. When they create unmitigated divisions in the local church, no. If the biblical image of the church is multiethnic, multigenerational, and multicultural, then the church should prize such diversities even in the midst of their difficulties, seeking always to bring the diverse elements of its community into unity through worship.[2]

The old can't be replaced by the new, whether it is a generational or cultural shift. Each informs and rounds out the other. Even communities of color are experiencing intergenerational divisions, and it is necessary to speak to the need for and steps to culture change. The young can't just disengage, and the old can't just ignore or judge. In "The Divide in the Black Church That Most Troubles Me," urban pastor Thabiti Anyabwile writes about a similar culture change within the black church:

It seems to me that the line between older and younger African-American Christians has never been deeper and wider. In fact, for increasing numbers of older and younger African-American Christians there's no real contact at all. . . .

An entire generation—the hip hop generation—has largely grown up without the formative shaping influences of the church. For many in this generation, the church seems quaint, a bit outdated and out of touch with their culture, energy and concerns. Some in this demographic see older saints as generally prejudiced against youth, resistant to their involvement, and perhaps even stuck in a bygone era so vastly different from their context as to be unrecognizable. . . .

Many from the hip hop generation want an ethos that not only reflects but celebrates hip hop sensibilities. They don't want to attend "grandmamma's church."[3]

RESPECTING LEGACY

Members of communities, including their leaders, who want to seek change must know *how* to approach change with humility and respect. Many of us who envision change are prone to rush change. We fail in effecting change because we wrongly attribute people's reasons for resistance. We also fail as change agents because we fail to respect the historical work behind the institution we want to change. We often hear new leaders declare that they are bringing ideas that will change the way things are done. It's as if they believe their presence alone will bring new and better results.

Several years ago I took over the leadership of a college student program that provided great opportunity for me to connect my love for worship, multicultural ministry, reconciliation and justice work. I was in my element. Simultaneously, I was attending an evangelical seminary known for its commitment to biblical scholarship. This was an exciting season of my life! I was able to pursue ministry while reflecting theologically on how we were approaching it. My seminary was also full of students who were much more conservative socially and politically than my urban Christian context. I was constantly being warned about the dangers of the social gospel spreading in the church, which gave me a close look at the fears people had about what we (those of us in justice work) were and were *not* saying. There was mistrust and confusion on both ends. I took seriously the fears and questions. I went back to the program curriculum and examined what we were teaching. Nothing was incorrect, but we cleared out buzzwords and language that might set off alarms. We adjusted the way things were stated for the current generation of millennials. Those changes had positive effects on the program, and the program flourished.

The next stage of change brought many alterations to the schedule, because the movement we were a part of was more strategically focused on the campus than ever before. The mission—global, urban, city work—would need to interact with the campus at a deeper level and equip students for the campus at a more strategic level. So, we made more curriculum changes, schedule changes and overall changes in form and function. We began to use different means of coaching staff and their directors in preparation for students returning to campus. The program flourished. I received a lot of feedback from campus leaders and partner sites about the "next level" the program had come to and how much "deeper" the theology was. It would have been tempting to take the credit for what we had done. By "we" I mean the college campus staff who came before me who had laid foundations for two decades. By "we" I mean the campus staff who were empowered to contribute to changes in the past decade (including myself as a young Latino staff).

The previous director had shared his leadership. The program was a collective work that had been in progress for twenty-five years. When I came, I brought my passions, my perspective and my gifts. I was proud of the work I had done and delighted to be respected for my contribution—who wouldn't be? The reality, however, was that I did not develop it from scratch. I was building on a legacy that included people who had mentored me. So as attractive as it would have been (and it was) to say, "Thanks, I just knew I could make it better" or "Oh no, shucks, I was just doing my best" (false humility), instead, I was honest. I shared my thankfulness for the previous director who had brought many of us onboard to consult, I thanked my seminary professors for scaring me into reflection, and I thanked the leaders who gave me feedback for noticing my unique, personal contributions. Five years later this program has a new staff team who will bring their own passions, personality and gifts. One of the new staff is an artist. She is fantastic with words, and God ministers to people through her spoken word. Another staff member has lived in Chicago his entire life (unlike any previous staff). I wonder how the culture might change as the younger leaders are empowered to create.

Many new or young leaders come with valuable ideas, but I'd like to give a word of caution: when we desire change we should communicate respect to our elders. This value is more dominant in communities of color, where hierarchy is important and age matters, but I share it as a gift to the white community as well. Newer is not always better, and newer that does not build on respect for history and previous foundations likely will not stick. Culture is dynamic, but it is created from a starting point and requires congregational buy-in of the inherited culture.

I recently had a conversation with a young pastor discouraged by the slow pace of change in his church. He said, "We need to get a new system in and tell the old ushers, 'You're not an usher anymore' and get 'em out. Or if the board doesn't want change, then we need to get a new one." The core issue is that change requires a process that involves the support of the whole community. Sure, it's easier to start from scratch. This is why some bloggers argue that the only way to have a multiethnic congregation is to plant one. They recommend starting with young people who are open to change, and developing the DNA from the beginning. Yes, this would be easier, but it is not the only way. And more importantly it leaves out a majority of churches and the generations that nurtured our faith. Fortune 500 companies that continue to grow regardless of current trends have leaders who adapt and graft in new ideas and people. The church is two thousand years old, so how have we adapted and changed? And where have we failed to change? What lasting principles anchor us while the cultural context and location demand change?

PREPARING THE GUESTS

Imagine a great breakfast! We sit at the breakfast table and notice that different cultures use distinct "spreads" for their toast: Latinos (dulce de leche), Europeans (Nutella), Aussies (Vegemite), and Americans (peanut butter). We may not realize that we're not open to change until someone swaps our dulce de leche for Vegemite!

Similarly, the first step in creating culture is understanding our own culture. Self-awareness helps us identify how our worship may be culturally located. What is our go-to spread that we reach for without thinking? If someone switched it without our knowledge, would we be angry? Why? We can help our community become aware of the cultural preferences we have by asking similar questions.

Second, before we judge our communities too harshly, we want to identify the reasons behind the resistance to change. It is important not to make assumptions. We might jump to the conclusion that people are ethnophobes, racists or too old-school for change based on particular markers. That would be a great disservice to our communities. I have seen people early in the journey attack their churches and communities before they've made changes themselves. Perhaps we spend a summer in an overseas slum, in the 'hood or exploring new ideas and are quick to indict our home churches for not caring enough about the poor, for allowing racism to linger unchecked or for not welcoming people who are different. We may be right, but we may be off. When people ask me what they can do to help their communities change, I tell them to (1) engage people in dialogue (this means listen too), (2) model in your own life what you want to see happening, and (3) invite people to join you. It's more effective to inspire people than rebuke them.

Once we've explored our own culture and suspended judgment regarding our congregation, we want to invite people to join us on a journey. We can start by sharing our own journey with the leader (e.g., pastor, worship team leader, ministry director), or ask him or her to begin the journey with us. Who are the major stakeholders in regard to worship? What group of people need to come alongside the vision for diverse worship? This may be a leadership team, elder board, staff team or worship team.

Given your interest, perhaps you already have experienced worship in different settings. My favorite way of learning is to visit churches different from my own. By being displaced in a community whose worship culture is not my own, I begin to understand the nuances in worship and community from church to church. When we want to prepare others for change, exposure is more effective than explanation. Expose your leadership to different traditions. This can be accomplished many different ways. For example:

- Expose leaders to worship from a different tradition.
    - Visit churches of different cultures and classes.
    - Participate in an event under the leadership of someone from a different culture.

o Collaborate on a crosscultural team.

o Lead worship in a church of a different culture and class. If you have a partnership, swap teams.

• Lead your team with the knowledge you already have.

o Share music and artists from a variety of backgrounds.

o Assign the team members articles, chapters or videos that expose them to other cultures.

o Share from your own experiences of worship and leading worship in diverse cultures.

o Uphold the values of those whom you have them read, learn from or listen to.

From Foodies to Family

We are a "foodie" generation. We see ourselves as diverse and enlightened because we are open to trying new foods. Sometimes those of us who are quick to change experience only surface change. We want multiethnic churches but are comfortable only when everyone is similar socioeconomically and in stage of life. We create spaces to welcome culturally different behaviors and symbols, but not deep values and concern. This is illustrated by the number of people in our country who speak Spanish, dance salsa and love Mexican food, but have no desire to explore the issues most relevant to our Latino churches (e.g., poor education in urban settings, family displacement and a broken immigration system). Leading worship in a multiethnic world requires hosts who can help our families enter into deeper communion with one another. How then do we influence our congregations? Consider the following:

• Connect change to the mission or big picture.

• Gather a group of stakeholders affected by the change. Have them work together.

- Get the buy-in of the leadership.

- Develop a vision of what things will look like in five years, and then communicate, communicate, communicate.

- Empower and help people to find their place and contribution.[4]

At Grace and Peace Community, where I pastor, the Lord's Supper was not consistently celebrated. We are a part of the Christian Reformed Church, which holds that the Lord's Supper is a sacrament that should be celebrated "normally and regularly as part of a single liturgy of Word and table."[5] We are also an urban church whose congregants come from Catholic and Pentecostal backgrounds; no one has roots in the CRC. With a desire to both esteem the Table as the centerpiece of worship while also understanding the context, I took small steps.

1. I conversed with the lead pastor to learn the history of the practice within our church, and observed the way we practiced it.

2. I administered it the same way, but began to add teaching from Scripture and the early church about the centrality of the Table.

3. I added a column to the preaching schedule (which I organize) to write in which weeks we'd celebrate the Lord's Supper.

4. I coordinated the celebration of the Table with a sermon passage that exalts Christ's life, death and resurrection.

5. When we had a sermon series from the book of Colossians, I asked the elders for permission to celebrate the Table weekly and explained to the congregation that it was to remind us of the theme of Colossians: the supremacy of Christ.

6. Instead of downplaying the imagery for fear of a negative response,[6] I highlighted the image by adorning a large table, setting fruit, pastries, breads and wine on it. I also used decanters and wine glasses. (It was actually grape juice, but it looks like wine.)

One of the church leaders expressed that as an artist, she really appreciated the attention I gave to the colors and artifacts as well as using food that was familiar to Latino culture. An African American male congregant said he was learning a lot about the power of biblical imagery from our times at the Table. The response has been positive. Ideally, we'd be celebrating the Table every week, given the instructions of Jesus and the practice of the first-century church, but the steps that seem small for me have felt earth shifting for others. In a local church these changes can take time, but patience is important for long-lasting change.

If changes in a local congregation require that much intentionality, system-wide changes in larger organizations require even more effort and at many levels. We need to identify the stakeholders and the existing structures that are ripe for change. At one denominational event I was planning worship for, the organizer told me he did not want me to lead worship the way he had seen me do it before. He showed me a chart similar to table 7.1.

Table 7.1. Differences Between Two Denominational Events

Past Event "X"	Current Event "Y"
Young people	Older people (50+)
Missional gathering	Fellowship gathering
Open to change	Skeptical of change
Diverse	Predominantly white (85%)

He said I could lead one "ethnic" song and three "normal" songs (hymns or contemporary), which is problematic. But beyond that he was clearly concerned about something else, so I asked. I found out that the previous year the worship had been led by an African American, and they received the following feedback on his leadership.

- "You don't have to scream at me to get me to worship."
- "Where are my hymns? Why can't we have more hymns?"
- "It was too loud. The music was too showy."
- "I don't like to be told what to do (dance, raise hand, etc.) during worship."

The organizer perceived that the issue was too much diversity, but the real issue was the *process* of diversification. When a congregation's normal worship is all European hymns led by a white leader and an organ, multicultural worship must be crafted with care. (The denominational event organizer also told me we *had* to use an organ.) He had a pastoral concern that needed to be taken seriously. The previous worship leader had missed the mark because he did not know how to adapt from his cultural norms. He is actually an excellent worship leader in his own context, but he failed to study the *normal* worship of the community in order to create a diverse worship space where they could encounter God.

As a Latina from an urban church I was not going to subject the attendees to three guitars and four percussion players, and cry the entire time I was leading worship. I had to honor them by knowing them first. I was able to convince the director that I could indeed lead the worshipers in a deeper model of multicultural worship that was accessible for the community. We mixed genres and used a healthy dose of hymns (arranged in parts and with an organ, piano and flute). We introduced new languages through familiar songs, readings and prayers representative of attendees, and led by attendees and leaders in their movement. We stretched them but didn't always scream at them. It was beautiful to watch the faces of the ethnic minority attendees as they saw their family genuinely engage the worship with hearts of openness.

After many hours of conversation with leaders involved in creating change, I am left with a few learning points.

- Interpret! Leaders serve as interpreters of an experience for their community. Changing culture requires us to explain the changes along the way, otherwise our silence is left to the wrong interpretation. Even if people don't like what we are doing, they will know what we are doing and why.

- Get feedback along the way. Leaders must pay attention to the dynamics of the congregation. Are they moving with us? We must also make sure we are listening to a variety of voices, and if we are intentionally trying to invite more ethnic minorities, we must pay special attention to their often marginalized voices. (In the case of the African American leader, I wonder if the people who were being listened to had access to the leaders, who are primarily white, and therefore were simply grieving that their preferences were not the focal point.)

- Be intentional about creating. It is fair for people to be wary if they are not sure who the leader is or what "church" they are at that week. This can become very confusing and disjointed even to people who value multiethnic worship. Each worshiping community must brand a specific style that makes sense for its context and use variety that is digestible.

Sometimes people get excited when they are exposed to a certain kind of worship and want to bring it back to their church. One young man was leading worship at an African American urban church context. His church was very familiar with a gospel (more fusion) song and had sung it many times. After coming back from a conference where he experienced global worship, he was leading this song and said, "Now we're going to sing it in Korean!" But there was no context for that change. There were no Koreans in their church. Most of the congregants had never met a Korean or been exposed to Korean culture. And the worship service was not a global missions celebration. In addition, there was nothing else

(Scripture, sermon, prayer) connected to global issues or Korea. I am sure the community was wondering why they were doing this, but unfortunately the young man never told them. They had a hard time engaging in the worship moment, and he never tried anything like that again.

At another event focused on solidarity with those on the margin, the well-meaning worship leader introduced a song by saying, "Now it's time to sing in French." Not one of the lines was translated into English, and no more was said. People seemed to enjoy watching the band sing the song, but there was little engagement from the community. An opportunity for transformation was missed because there was no connection to the topic of the conference. Imagine if they had explained that French is spoken in specific African countries, shared a statement about the issues of oppression within that context and explained the main message of the song? Inviting the community to connect might have modeled for people what changes can move us to deeper worship. It was also interesting to speak to a worship team member who was French speaking, but was not empowered to lead, and who said he was actually embarrassed by the experience.

Assuming these worship leaders wanted to expose the church to global worship and God's concern for the world, what else could they have done? How could they have prepared the congregation for the experience? Where could the songs have been placed?

Communities are not always ready for multiethnic worship. On one occasion I was asked to lead worship for a church service in Wisconsin. This church was predominantly white (maybe 2 percent minority). When I was working with the technical person to upload lyrics, he said, "Oh good, I see we are singing in Chinese. We have some oriental people in our church." When I heard the term *oriental*, which is offensive to Asian and Asian American people, I took that as a cue that this was not the place to lead that song. Seeing that the church was using a term about two-to-three decades behind the time, the church leadership clearly had not had exposure to that particular community. It was better to go for some low-hanging fruit.

Most of us dislike change. We are wary of new ideas, particularly if they threaten our sense of normalcy or identity. This is not an issue for only white people, white churches or older Christians who can't accept modern worship. This is an issue for all of us. Having worked for over a decade in creating multiethnic worship experiences with dozens of communities, most of my exposure was with white and multiethnic congregations, primarily white-Asian suburban or upper-middle-class college-educated people. I began to internalize that it was just majority folks or people in power who were not open to new things. But the more I worked with urban African American and Latino churches, I realized we all fear change. I was working with a church that had just transitioned from having a white worship leader with a formal liturgical background. She was a gifted musician whose style came out even when she led more contemporary music. (She also followed the church calendar.) When I began to work with them, I suggested that we do something special for Advent. It was as if I had said dirty word. "Advent?" the leader said. "Oh, we don't do that stuff here. That's for white people." They had associated ancient church traditions with a particular style and they had no desire to assimilate.

CULTURE CREATORS

All of us feel called to different places of influence. While many of us are trying to change culture from within an existing structure, others are trying to do something completely new. We can redeem and create culture. Makoto Fujimura, artist and author on the arts, calls us to see ourselves as stewards of culture and to take responsibility to shape the culture all around us. He writes, "Culture is not a territory to be won or lost but a resource we are called to steward with care. Culture is a garden to be cultivated."[7]

Let's look at three communities of pastors and artists who are writing their own music and liturgies that display their commitment to multiethnicity, reconciliation and mission. They are different examples of communities seeking to create new cultures of worship.

Josh Davis, coauthor of *Worship Together in Your Church as in Heaven*, directs Proskuneo, which "exists to glorify God [and] promote unity in the body of Christ through multilingual multicultural worship gatherings, worship resources, and training in order that lives be transformed and nations come together to worship God."[8] He hosts a year-round school of the arts in Clarkston, Georgia, where three-fourths of the population is estimated to be foreign born and together speaks over sixty languages. He also runs the Proskuneo Worship Institute (thepwi.info), which is a month-long experience of learning about multiethnic worship in diverse community.

David Bailey is the director of Arrabon, a ministry in Richmond, Virginia, providing worship resources "created out of the experiences of living and worshipping together in a diverse community of believers."[9] Arrabon cohosts the Urban Songwriting Internship, which is an intensive eight-week program offered in partnership with East End Fellowship. Interns not only learn about multicultural worship and planning worship in the urban context, they also spend time writing songs that develop from their studies and time as a community.

Jaewoo Kim is director of Arts in Mission Korea (artmissionkorea .wordpress.com), which equips Korean and Korean-diaspora artists for crosscultural ministries. He also directs King's Region, which is a Dallas-based Korean diaspora worship-arts ministry. Jay is creating worship experiences that expose people to God's heart for mission.

They are not necessarily focused on songwriting, but on bringing awareness to the Korean church of the importance of multicultural worship and mission.

I know myself. I have a vision of what could be and I want people to get there. I have made my share of mistakes, made assumptions about people's intentions and burnt instead of built bridges in my quest for change. As we see in the Scriptures, God exercises patience with his people as they follow him. May we do the same as we desire to move our congregations to God's global table.

KEY CONCEPTS

- When introducing change, it's important to acknowledge those who've gone before us.
- Preparing people for change requires intentionality. It's not something that can be done on our own but needs the involvement of the whole community.
- Patience is important for long-lasting change.

FOR REFLECTION

- Does your approach and attitude to change honor the gifts God has already given to the community you are a part of? If so, how have you communicated honor to the community?
- Does your desire for change divide the community into us-versus-them? How have you included and involved the stakeholders of your community?

FOR DISCUSSION

- As you move your fellowship to multiethnic worship, how can you best engage the leaders and elders of your community?

- What is the worship legacy of your community? How can that be celebrated and integrated into your journey of multiethnic worship?

- Plan to lead a new song as part of a worship service. How can you prepare the congregation? What elements besides the song itself can help facilitate this?

Prayer. God, humble us. Give us eyes to see the gifts you have given our fellowship. May we be able to give honor to those who have gone before us and creatively dream about where we are going. And move in our midst that we would be open to grow in our worship of you, the God of all peoples.

eight

MASTER CHEF

Training Worship Leaders

Training worship leaders has been my single most exciting mission of the past fifteen years. These men and women come with many creative ideas and the desire to see others develop deeper communion with the Lord. The most common question I am asked by leaders is, "How do I grow as a worship leader?" The second is similar, "How do I develop other worship leaders?" Across generations, genders and ethnicities, these questions burn in people's hearts. The problem is that most of our training, schooling and books on leadership are focused on the first question. Very little in my career, including seminary, trained me to train leaders. This was the single greatest gift I received while being on staff with InterVarsity. We didn't merely lead Bible studies or speak; we developed leaders and preachers. This is the foundation of my worship ministry and my work as a pastor. I spend my energy on the need to raise future generations of leaders for the church. In the same way a master chef learns to cook, display food and create a great restaurant environment, worship leaders require training for their journey. The process of developing leaders starts with our individual leadership; we can teach others what we have learned. A prospective chef first learns the basics of cooking and then learns to cook from books. Next, the chef perfectly duplicates great creations of others, and finally experiments with his or her own creations. This chapter will illustrate this process of leadership development primarily through the journey and relationships of others.

GROWTH TAKES TIME

Cooking is something I enjoy. There is no style of food that I will not experiment with. Having grown up with a Latina mom, I was stirring and chopping by the time I was five. I now can make many delicious Colombian and Argentine dishes. I can also make some mean Americanized tacos complete with iceberg lettuce and El Paso hard shells. (Our poor family did not know any Mexicans early on, so we learned from TV commercials.) In my neighborhood we can get great food from anywhere south of the border (Puerto Rican, Mexican, Cuban, Colombian), but the Chinese offered is awful. I don't live anywhere near Chinatown, so I had to learn to cook Chinese food. I already knew the basics of cooking, and I had some recipes for my favorite foods, so I began a five-year journey in the art of Chinese cuisine. My friends Gerald and Vivian taught me that a meal consists of three meats; therefore having a good knife matters. My friends Krystle and Won taught me that dark meat is better than white meat, and that having the right marinades is important. Though my friends have cooked with us almost a dozen times, when I cook by myself it's edible, but not delicious. I asked my husband why he thought I couldn't get it right, and he reminded me that I didn't have two decades of watching my mom and being her sous-chef.

As in cooking, worship leadership takes emotional intelligence, skills and coaching.

EMOTIONAL INTELLIGENCE AND SELF-AWARENESS

Leading others in worship and in change takes emotional intelligence and self-awareness. The more aware we are about ourselves and our cultures, the easier it is to identify the disconnect for the people we are trying to bring into a new experience. There is no reason to judge ourselves or our cultures, for example thinking we are too emotional or our worship is boring. However, being aware of who we are and what influences us will help us become socially and culturally competent. Knowing our strengths, personality and spiritual gifts will help us lead more effectively.

According to the Myers-Briggs Type Indicator (myersbriggs .org), I am an ENFP (extraverted, intuitive, feeler, perceiver).[1] I have strengths in communication and gathering input or information, and a gift in teaching and leadership. I love to dream with people about what could be. I read books, speak with people, try new things, read some more and propose ideas. Everything is process at all times. I envision a future of possibilities and seek to inspire people to imagine with me. I struggle with closure and structure.[2] Knowing these things about myself allows me to own and celebrate who God has made me. This knowledge also makes me alert and sensitive to my weaknesses, my need for others and others' perceptions of me.

One of my close colleagues, Melissa Vallejo, is different from me. In her leadership as an INTP (introverted, intuitive, thinker, perceiver), she has strengths in executing and strategic thinking, and a gift in administration. She excels at developing structures that hold things together. As an introvert, her most significant contributions are not seen but felt. She establishes processes that create environments of collaboration. She is a percussionist, which means she is precise! Melissa has produced many worship CDs and is able to get musical results from people because she pays close attention to how crisp the sound is. She brings her keen observation and analytical skills to her work as a pastor and worship leader. But she struggles with on-the-spot transitions in worship and needs time to prepare. She too is aware of her strengths and weaknesses.

Sometimes awareness hurts. Becky, an Asian woman, had a powerful worship ministry. She was a gifted musician, pastor and prophet. She was versatile in her style and was able to lead people in passionate, Spirit-filled worship. But when an event she led was recorded, she was shocked by what she heard. She realized she sounded more like a Disney character than Aretha Franklin or Beyoncé. She was an excellent singer, so this discovery did not mean she was less qualified for her calling. However, she became aware of what her voice sounded like to others and subsequently worked on developing a lower register and tone. That experience was critical for her growth.

Leaders who are intuitive about people and spaces may have an easier time becoming self-aware, but all of us need to grow in this area. There are tools and assessments we can take to analyze and invest in our leadership, such as Myers-Briggs, StrengthsFinder, spiritual gift assessments, DISC and emotional intelligence evaluation. Lack of self-awareness or social (or cultural) awareness on the part of a leadership team will affect the worship experience of the community. This is particularly true when working crossculturally.

Tom, a white male, was working in an African American community. He had received feedback that it was hard for them to trust him. Although he has great friendships within the African American community, two particular women did not feel comfortable around him. He came from affluence, and the ways he dressed, talked and behaved triggered their previous negative experiences. He was not necessarily doing anything wrong, but the symbols he embodied were barriers for the women (and likely for others). He was asked by a mentor to consider dressing differently and not taking notes on his laptop during his conversations with others. He felt he was being asked to not be himself. While he is entitled to freedom of expression, since it was creating barriers for him he decided to be more flexible and to empty himself. There are dozens of ways that we may alter our personal expression to cross cultures more effectively. Reconciliation calls us to be a Greek to Greeks and a Jew to Jews (1 Corinthians 9:20). Due to cultural displacement, people of color in North America may have a better understanding than others of how the ways we dress, speak and act affect others since they are not part of the dominant culture.

Leaders who want to develop crosscultural competency should begin with emotional intelligence, which is the ability to be in touch with our emotions and manage them. We should learn the skills to read ourselves and our surroundings and be able to manage perceptions. This is a particularly valuable skill when crossing cultures. Consider how you may grow in recognizing and regulating yourself (see fig. 8.1).[3] Which area might be hard for you?

	SELF	SOCIAL
Recognition	**Self-Awareness** **Self-confidence** emotional self-awareness accurate self-assessment	**Social Awareness** **Empathy** organizational awareness understanding the environment
Regulation	**Self Management** **Self-control** trustworthiness conscientiousness adaptability drive and motivation initiative	**Social Skills** **Influence** inspirational leadership developing others building bonds teamwork and collaboration

Figure 8.1. Four elements of emotional intelligence theory

When crossing cultures, worship leaders must be aware of how preferences are experienced by others. This can be as simple as being aware of our singing voice and musical instincts. I've worked with many nonblack vocalists in altering the intonation and pronunciation of their singing so they don't sound stiff or formal when singing black gospel or African songs. I say, for example,

- "Give me something earthier."
- "Less pretty, more growl."
- "Move while you sing. It will help you feel the natural bounce of the song."
- "Smile and sing it."
- "Try 'I can't leeve' and not 'I can't live.' Make it a double *e*."

An African American male I work with always tells me, "Make it more chocolatey, Sandra." He is referring to my pronunciation and my intonation, and would like to hear more ad-libs and runs. He is trying to help me authenticate the style of the song. However, if I am trying to authenticate a hymn or CCM song, I would *not* make it chocolatey (unless, of course, I am intentionally making a fusion arrangement). This means that if I ask urban Latino or African American vocalists to simplify their vocals and sing the actual melody, they may feel stifled. I was once working with a Latina who said it did not feel natural to her to sing the CCM chorus the way I was asking her to. I responded that it was not natural for our Asian American brother to sing in Spanish and play the guitar the way we were asking him to. It took him months to learn the riffs we needed for our song. "Ohhhh," she responded. She got it. Crossing cultures, learning new languages and adding new styles of music is unnatural to all of us.

COACHING LEADERS

It is important to know where our musicians and leaders are coming from. Do they tend toward one genre? What preferences do they have? I once worked with a musical director whose expertise was jazz, so our cumbia and salsa sounded more like Latin jazz. It was cool, but not correct. It made me upset, like when my husband puts *chile y limon* in my Colombian rice, thus making it Mexican. Having good coaches for ourself as well as the leaders we are seeking to develop is critical. I regularly hired African American musical directors and Latino instrumentalists to pair up with my leaders. They would train and workshop our teams. Who do you have coaching and training you and your leaders? Can you have someone come in to work with your vocalists, band or leaders?

The coaching often includes more than music. Karen, a young woman I was working with for a weeklong camp, felt uncomfortable when I asked her to move more when she led worship. She was singing the notes beautifully and pronouncing the Spanish with expertise, but standing in one place with a closed, understated posture. Latino worship leaders stand with open hands and open arms, and use the entire stage (and aisles if they need more space). They use their entire bodies in worship. To convey the essence and passion of Latino worship, merely singing the notes well was not going to cut it. I spent the afternoon running around the room, gesturing and asking for eye contact from every corner. I wanted her to personally connect with each person in the room. I looked foolish jumping around, pretending to be in the audience trying to attract her attention for almost an hour, but in the end she provided an authentic worship experience for the community. The cultural gap between a reserved Midwestern white girl and an urban Latino was a hard one to cross, but Karen did a fantastic job embodying the gifts of that style.

Breaking our worship-leading habits can be hard. The following is the story of Andy Kim, a Korean American worship leader I have coached over the years:

> "Andy, I'd like to you lead this gospel song, but put down the guitar and just sing."
>
> Dumbfounded, I looked at my staffworker. "But Sandra, without a guitar I feel . . . so . . . naked." At the moment I couldn't put words to my strong reaction to her seemingly simple request, but without my guitar I felt exposed, vulnerable and, yes, naked.
>
> I was reluctant to put away my guitar. I would have never dared to say it out loud, but I felt that my worship would be hindered without my guitar. My unwillingness to put down my guitar betrayed a deeper mindset: an unwillingness to sacrifice my own preferences in worship. I wanted to lead others on my own terms, in ways that were safe and secure for me. And if this was truly the case, I wondered, how else was I subconsciously expecting others to enter into God's presence on my terms?
>
> Without the guitar, I was suddenly free to interact with the congregation. I didn't have to think about which chord to play next but rather worship with them in a more interactive way. And then it struck me: this is perhaps one of the reasons why we rarely see a worship leader in the gospel tradition lead on an instrument, so they can exhort and interact with the congregation! What previously was awkward and foreign suddenly became a wonderful, fresh and new way of worshiping God and leading others in worship. I would have never arrived at those insights had Sandra not challenged me to put down the guitar. Simply put, I would have never grown in my view of worship or as a worship leader had I not been willing to get naked.[4]

Andy serves as a multiethnic resource specialist for InterVarsity and has produced a series of training videos on multiethnic worship that help communities enter into diverse forms of worship.[5]

Worship leaders also need coaching and development in theology. Theology is caught via worship. Justo González says, "Too often the theme of worship is excluded or set aside from theological matters, when in fact theology and praise, doctrine and worship, are so interwoven that if we separate them they both lose much of their significance and value."[6] An Old Testament professor shocked me by stating that the worship leader is the primary person who shapes the theology of the congregation. Ben Shin, professor of New Testament at Biola University, echoed these same concerns, saying, "More than the Bible, our young millennials' theology is being shaped by music. Because social media is the way to get music, the message goes far and wide. They just access it all the time on their phones, so they can quote a song more than the verse of the Bible."[7] Since many worship leaders are not theologians but musicians who happen to pastor, there is reason to have concern.

PASTORING EGO

It is common for worship leaders to struggle with performance and ego. Given the current worship music industry, it's hard not to fall into the trap of wanting to be famous or popular. In a shared-leadership setting, the temptation to compare ourselves to others is great. The desire to stand out, be the best singer and exercise the most spiritual authority can be strong. Audrey Tom, a worship leader in San Diego, says,

> When you're on stage in front of a crowd, large or small, you all of a sudden become *known*. And let's be honest: any of us that has the nature of a performer, an artist, or an influencer also has a hungry ego. We like being known. We like being

affirmed. We like feeling useful. We like feeling important and recognized. We like feeling like we have something to offer. We like displaying our gifts, and we especially like being admired for them. It's okay, I can admit it, and so can you. We are broken and sinful and in need of God's grace and redemption. But as such, let's not be naive to understand that for us the stage can be dangerous territory, giving us and our hungry egos a complex if we are not careful.

How easy it is to bask in all the people that now know us, all of the praise we get for a job well done, all of the thanks we get for touching someone's life, and all the admiration we receive for our gifts. And how easy it is to feed our hungry little egos that say, "Look at me! I'm so important! I'm so awesome! I'm talented, really I am!" Honestly, I don't think it's completely wrong to want to be known, loved, or affirmed. We all need a little encouragement, and we all need to receive love. But as worship leaders, our job is to lead people in worshipping and glorifying the Lord, and when we crave that attention for ourselves, then it is no longer about glorifying God, rather we've made it about glorifying ourselves. Instead of genuinely working for God to be worshipped and glorified we are secretly working for affirmation and praise—for *us* to be glorified, for *us* to seem important, and for *us* to seem worthy of something. For a worship leader, that's not okay.

Like we said, there is no room for egos here.[8]

The first thing that will help control our ego is being confident in our strengths and our true self. This confidence will give us the courage to try new things and to empty ourself when we need to adapt.

The second thing that will help is understanding our weaknesses. I know that I am not a strong band leader. My strengths are being a vocalist and pastor. Therefore, whenever I take on complicated projects, I hire a musical director to help me with charting the music and the band. There is no reason for me to get insecure, because I know that what I offer as a crosscultural coach and pastor benefits my team. I know who I am and I know what I need. Ego issues typically arise when musicians and leaders are insecure and feel the need to prove themselves or one-up someone else. This is not helpful in building collaboration on a team. It is especially unhelpful if the overall leader of the team is not confident and secure. It makes it difficult for them to share leadership and celebrate the people they are leading.

It is also important for leaders to know their leadership limitations. I strongly advise against moving people into leadership before they are ready. This may be particularly hard when diversity is lacking and a young leader with potential is available who could contribute to the team. This may be most difficult for the young person who knows he or she is not ready to lead. Remember, timing is everything. A good worship leader is a mature Christian whose growth must not be compromised by a particular need on a worship team. More harm than good can happen. When sharing leadership it is also important to know the various leaders' limitations. Leading a congregation of one hundred is not the same as leading five thousand. The skills, confidence and presence required are different. Not everyone on a team is gifted or destined for large arenas or sanctuaries of worshipers. You yourself may not be gifted or destined for certain roles of leadership. It is important to be confident in your calling, whatever that calling is.

We shouldn't be afraid to apprentice young leaders by entrusting them with roles that fit their stage of growth, and empowering them to lead and take measured risks. Samuel Barreto, a worship pastor in Chicago, is known for taking young musicians under his wing and training them as artists as well as mentoring them spiritually.

I have met many worship leaders and musicians who express gratitude for the time Sam gave to them. Imagine my joy when Sam came to work at Grace and Peace; I was thrilled to have him on my pastoral team. In just a few years we went from having no youth on our worship ministry team to having all of the tech functions overseen by youth and a strong youth presence on our worship team and in the choir.

How might you identify artists among your young people? You might not start them off on a Sunday morning, but are there other services or places where you might begin to take risks? With sufficient coaching and preparation a team of worship leaders can be developed in a few years.

LEAD WORSHIPER VERSUS WORSHIP LEADER

There is a myth that the worship leader is merely a lead worshiper. While this sounds nice, it's simply not true. It is true that the heart, posture and focus of the song leader must be worshipful. The integrity and attitude of a worship leader is central. In this generation and culture more than ever our integrity as a leader is the key to our influence. Life integrity—how we are leading off stage—communicates loudly to the congregation in intangible ways. Worship leaders must practice the spiritual disciplines in order to stay sensitive to the Holy Spirit, not only for direction in mission but for conviction of sin. However, the worship leader's job goes beyond lead worshiper. There are three relationships the worship leader is responsible for: (1) *communion with God*, the Spirit's leading and conviction in both planning for and during the service, (2) *attentiveness to the congregation*, and (3) *connection to the team* as the one who is guiding the time. It can be a train wreck when the worship leader is focused on self and not aware of the three relationships. This is especially important when leading worship crossculturally, since misreading cues is a possibility (e.g., the congregation is not in it). This has happened when African Americans, for example, lead Asian Americans, who do not express themselves as African Americans do. It can also happen when we think team members are in line with our vision, but in reality their values do not allow them to challenge our leadership.

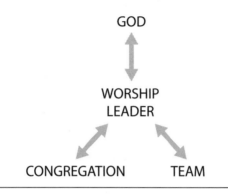

Figure 8.2

The worship leader serves as a host, guide or interpreter of the experience. This is a critical skill a worship leader must develop. A concrete philosophy of worship allows leaders to pastor the community in such a way that they learn to value multiethnic worship. Leaders must ask what they want people to understand, feel and do.

Attentiveness to the new experience for the community is imperative. A worship leader can make a thoughtful thirty- to sixty-second statement that helps the congregation with the new worship experience. I always prepare my leaders for the opening of a set when we lead multiethnic worship in a church unaccustomed to such diversity. One time we were leading a diverse-worship set in a large, predominantly white Presbyterian church in Los Angeles. I suggested that the worship leader should explain to the congregation why a Korean woman was leading a white congregation in black gospel. Rather than saying something off-the-cuff like, "Oh, this is odd and kind of cool," we came up with a great interpretive statement that would move the congregation to a deeper place.

This must be done for everyone, not only for white congregations, since everyone has an ethnicity and culture. At a conference for a historically European denomination I started a session by holding up a hymnal. I asked if anyone had ever seen one. They all laughed. I continued, "Hymnals are deep, theological treatises. Long ago, church folks put theology to popular music so that people would learn about God. This is how I began my theological journey. At First Baptist Church I was introduced to God by hymnal and organ. What a blessed way to begin." I then shared about the song we were gong to start with. I am sure they were very shocked to find out that this woman who had been singing in so many languages (and dancing and sweating) knew and was blessed by traditional hymns. I wanted to say, "I love your language. I understand it and celebrate with it, but it's not 'normal' worship. It's an ethnic form of worship like gospel, Native American and so on." When we interpret ethnic minority or global forms of worship but not white worship, we contrast it with "normal" worship and pigeonhole ethnic minorities as "other." In church settings we have more time to interpret and teach our community. We are shaping our worshiping community over the long haul. But in more produced settings, our effort needs to be reduced to thirty to ninety seconds!

The more aware worship leaders are of their own preferences and the culture in which they are leading, the more successful they will be in developing a new culture of worship. Their journey will consist of shedding ego and taking risks.

Rev. Gail Song Bantum, executive pastor of Quest Church in Seattle, is a developer of leaders. She has been a multiethnic worship leader for many years and says that one of the defining moments in her own leadership was recognizing that she was placed in this world to collaborate with others. Many people in her congregation and on her staff affirm that she has the ability to see potential in others. Early in her worship leading Gail became aware of what she was good and not so good at. Though she is a trained musician, she does not consider herself a singer, so she relies on others to contribute their voices and other gifts. Sharing her leadership was easier when she understood she needed help— that adding other gifts in part creates greater potential for the whole. When I asked Pastor Gail why collaboration and developing leaders is so important to worship, she said we need one another. Since early on she studied classical music and conducting, she interpreted leadership in those terms:

> An orchestra conductor's back is always turned to the audience. They are definitively the leader—very present, front and center, influencing and directing—but the faces that you see from the audience are the instrumentalists. A conductor needs the gifts and presence of the players. The nature of a conductor's position is such that she cannot work alone. I need them to play what is in my head, what I hear, what I envision.

This brilliant image of leadership allows her to shape and create space for others to use their leadership gifts, allowing other voices to be cultivated.

As the former worship leader at Quest, a church committed to diversity, Gail developed a vision for worship that sought to be authentic to the community. She started by building trust and entering into the existing worship culture. Then she began teaching and casting vision with her worship team, helping them to see the importance of diverse worship. As someone who's been profoundly formed in the Pentecostal black church tradition, Gail began coaching the instrumentalists in embracing and understanding gospel music (syncopated beats, etc.). She invited them to feel the music so the song became a part of them. The vocalists were trained not only in their parts but were asked, "When we get to the 'ohs,' what are you going to do with them?" She coached them, explaining that the "ohs" were cries of desperation (when there's nothing left to say) coming from the lived experience of the African American community. Gail developed the worship team and its leaders so well that when she became the executive pastor, others were ready to lead in her place. Imagine if each of us considered working ourselves out of a job by training leaders who could succeed us.

Key Concepts

- Self-awareness is a foundational growth area for all leaders, but especially when crossing cultures in diverse worship.
- Feedback is a necessary part of the development of worship leaders.
- Acknowledge your weaknesses and engage others to help compliment your skill sets.
- The threefold role of a worship leader is to commune to God, be attentive to the congregation and connect with the team.

For Reflection

- Who are you getting feedback from? What are they saying about your leadership?
- What areas of worship leading are you not gifted in? Who can you work with to counter those deficiencies?

For Discussion

- How do we develop leaders in our congregation?
- Of the three roles of a worship leader, what is our focus? Why are all three important?

EPILOGUE

North Park University

North Park University, a Christian liberal arts university founded by the Evangelical Covenant Church, is located in one of the most diverse neighborhoods on the north side of Chicago. The student body of about 3,700 students is 25 percent students of color (approximately one-third black, Latino and Asian). Over the past decade the University Ministries office has pursued creating an environment that includes students from every ethnicity and culture in their worship services and programs. African American worship arts director Steve Kelly has been leading students in the difficult task of creating a culture of hospitality, solidarity and mutuality. He has selected an approach to shared leadership (multiethnic team ownership), identified models of diverse worship that work in their context (blended), and developed leaders and teams to create a new culture of worship. What has their journey been like?

When Stephen came to North Park, having served as a worship leader in a south-side African American church and as a musical director at Willow Creek Church, North Park's chapel was already experimenting with multicultural worship. It included some diversity in style of music and team leadership. Stephen's first task was to teach his students and cast vision for the underlying values of multiethnic worship. He wanted to "create an environment where people from all walks of life can engage with God," where no one culture would be put above the beauty of the body, and students learned to submit their preferences of how they see God to a more holistic picture of God.[1]

Next, Stephen needed worship leaders. He wanted not only diverse representation but people he could empower. He started with a group of students who were willing to learn. Musicality was important, but the biggest challenge was getting the students to submit to one another. In the first few years Stephen was more heavily involved in orchestrating worship because students trusted him but had a harder time trusting one another. Stephen wanted to help his worship teams be more integrated. He hoped they would step into each other's lives and stories in ways that make worship authentic .

Today, North Park chapel worship comprises three multiethnic teams led by multiple leaders. They all work together (including Stephen) to select song packages for the year as well as develop the worship sets for the weekly gatherings. They choose songs based on the following parameters: the group identifies with the song, it works with the theme, there is overall diversity (with a focus on black gospel and Spanish/bilingual songs). Stephen is a pianist, organist and musical director. As he works with his teams, he sometimes has to let the music be what it is so he can focus on the heart of worship. They have had great success as a team, and the students attending chapel have begun to enter into each other's story.

There are still areas where Stephen would like to see growth. He'd like to work with his leaders to pastor the moments of worship. He'd also love to explore moving from a blended model week to week to a collaborative rotation model so the congregation can be invited more often by different communities into a deeper narrative (see chap. 5). They have done this during Black History and Hispanic Heritage months, but more can be done to enter into the authentic experiences of different communities. Students who attend North Park return to their home churches as change agents who have experienced hospitality, solidarity and mutuality in worship. They shape the culture of the churches to which they return.

Multiethnic worship acknowledges and honors the diversity of people in the local and global church, and teaches congregations to understand and honor that same diversity. Through the expressions and themes of congregational worship, the call to unity is taken seriously. In the next season we must develop resources that help us create congregational worship experiences that connect us with the whole church. At the table we foster reconciliation, inviting and including each other, sharing leadership, and allowing all God's people to worship together regardless of our backgrounds.

My prayer is that you will explore approaches, forms and styles of worship for the future of the church—the next worship.

CULTURAL VALUES CONTINUUM

Write "S" above the number that best reflects yourself, "G" above the number that best reflects the values of your ethnic group and "C" above the number that best reflects your Christian community as a whole.

Direct communication   Indirect communication

1—————————————————————————————10

Emotions expressed   Emotions restrained

1—————————————————————————————10

Relationship follows task   Task follows relationship

1—————————————————————————————10

Identity from self   Identity from community

1—————————————————————————————10

Rules are universal   Rules vary based on context

1—————————————————————————————10

Change environment   Adapt to environment
1——————————————————————————————10

Status from accomplishment   Status from position
1——————————————————————————————10

Clock time   Event time
1——————————————————————————————10

DEFINITIONS

Communication.
Direct communication: Spoken and written words should stand on their own and be clear without additional subtext.
Indirect communication: Nonverbal communication and subtext communicate as much as what is actually said.

Emotions.
Emotions expressed: Honoring others means disclosing the nature and intensity of your internal responses.
Emotions restrained: Honoring others means controlling the nature and intensity of your internal responses.

Trust.
Relationship follows task: Bonds are first built through shared tasks, and we trust that relationships will follow.
Task follows relationship: Bonds are first built through relating, and we trust that tasks will follow.

Identity.
Identity from self: Integrity means knowing and being true to yourself.
Identity from community: Integrity means knowing and being true to your community.

Rules.

Rules are universal: The best rules should apply to everyone all the time. Authority means you get to determine the rules.

Rules vary based on context: The best rules flex according to circumstances. Authority means you get to decide exceptions to the rules.

Relating to environment.

Change environment: Effectiveness is determined by how much you can change your environment.

Adapt to environment: Effectiveness is determined by how much you can adapt to different environments.

Status.

Status from accomplishment: Influence and honor are accorded based on what you have produced, especially recently.

Status from position: Influence and honor are accorded based on title, seniority or long-term experience.

Time.

Clock time: Activities begin and conclude based on fixed start and end points.

Event time: Start and end points are defined by when the previous activity concludes and the subsequent activity begins.

Appendix B

ADDITIONAL RESOURCES

Books on Race and Culture

Cleveland, Christena (social psychologist). *Disunity in Christ: Uncovering the Hidden Forces That Keep Us Apart.* Downers Grove, IL: InterVarsity Press, 2013.

DeYmaz, Mark, and Harry Li (pastors). *Leading a Healthy Multi-Ethnic Church: Seven Common Challenges and How to Overcome Them.* Leadership Network Innovation Series. Grand Rapids: Zondervan, 2013.

DeYoung, Curtiss Paul, Michael O. Emerson, George Yancey and Karen Chai Kim (sociologists). *United by Faith: The Multiracial Congregation as an Answer to the Problem of Race.* New York: Oxford University Press, 2004.

Elmer, Duane (missiologist). *Cross-Cultural Conflict: Building Relationships for Effective Ministry.* Downers Grove, IL: InterVarsity Press, 1993.

Plueddemann, James E. (missiologist). *Leading Across Cultures: Effective Ministry and Mission in the Global Church.* Downers Grove, IL: InterVarsity Press, 2009.

Salter McNeil, Brenda (theologian). *Roadmap to Reconciliation: Moving Communities into Unity, Wholeness and Justice.* Downers Grove, IL: InterVarsity Press, 2015.

Salter McNeil, Brenda (theologian), and Rick Richardson (missiologist). *The Heart of Racial Justice: How Soul Change Leads to Social Change.* Expanded ed. Downers Grove, IL: InterVarsity Press, 2009.

BOOKS ON WORSHIP

Blount, Brian K., and Leonora Tubbs Tisdale (theologians). *Making Room at the Table: An Invitation to Multicultural Worship.* Louisville, KY: Westminster John Knox, 2001.

Cherry, Constance M. (pastor). *The Worship Architect: A Blueprint for Designing Culturally Relevant and Biblically Faithful Services.* Grand Rapids: Baker Academic, 2010.

Davis, Josh, and Nikki Lerner (practitioners). *Worship Together in Your Church as in Heaven.* Nashville: Abingdon, 2015.

González, Catherine Gunsalus (bilingual theologian). *Resources in the Ancient Church for Today's Worship / Lecciones del culto antiguo para la iglesia de hoy.* Nashville: Abingdon, 2014.

Kauflin, Bob (pastor). *Worship Matters: Leading Others to Encounter the Greatness of God.* Wheaton, IL: Crossway, 2008.

Krabill, James R. (missiologist), general ed. *Worship and Mission for the Global Church: An Ethnodoxology Handbook.* Pasadena, CA: William Carey Library, 2013.

Labberton, Mark (theologian). *The Dangerous Act of Worship: Living God's Call to Justice.* Downers Grove, IL: InterVarsity Press, 2007.

Marti, Gerardo (sociologist). *Worship Across the Racial Divide: Religious Music and the Multiracial Congregation.* New York: Oxford University Press, 2012.

Maynard-Reid, Pedrito U. (missiologist). *Diverse Worship: African-American, Caribbean and Hispanic Perspectives.* Downers Grove, IL: InterVarsity Press, 2000.

Webber, Robert E. (theologian). *Worship Old and New.* Grand Rapids: Zondervan, 1994.

Yee, Russell (pastor). *Worship on the Way: Exploring Asian North American Christian Experience.* Valley Forge, PA: Judson Press, 2012.

WEBSITES

Arrabon: http://arrabon.com

Calvin Institute of Christian Worship: http://worship.calvin.edu

InterVarsity Multiethnic Ministries: http://mem.intervarsity.org/mem
/resources

InterVarsity "Diverse Worship Matters" videos: https://vimeo.com/119363874
(summary); https://vimeo.com/115291470 (video 1); https://vimeo
.com/116011233 (video 2); https://vimeo.com/117637951 (video 3)

Proskuneo Ministries: http://proskuneo.org

Urbana 12 Worship blog: https://urbana.org/blog/urbana-12-worship

NETWORKING

International Council of Ethnodoxologists: www.worldofworship.org

Mosaix Global Network: www.mosaix.info

Multicultural Worship Leaders Network (MWLN) Facebook group:
www.facebook.com/groups/115159921876519/

Appendix C

WORSHIP MOVEMENTS AND ARTISTS

Table C.1

Artist/Movement	Style	Website
Fred Hammond	Black Gospel	www.realfredhammond.com
Kirk Franklin	Black Gospel	www.kirkfranklin.com
Shekinah Glory	Black Gospel	https://itunes.apple.com/us/artist/shekinah-glory-ministry/id258737458
VaShawn Mitchell	Black Gospel	http://vashawnmitchell.com
Eddie James	Black Gospel Crossover	www.ejworship.org
Israel Houghton	Black Gospel Crossover	http://newbreedmusic.com
William McDowell	Black Gospel Crossover	www.williammcdowellmusic.com
Tye Tribbett	Black Gospel/Rock	www.myplaydirect.com/tye-tribbett
Chris Tomlin	CCM	www.christomlin.com/home
Gateway Worship	CCM	http://gatewayworship.com
Hillsong	CCM	http://hillsong.com/worship
Passion	CCM	www.worshiptogether.com/partners/passion
The Brilliance	CCM/Americana	http://thebrilliancemusic.com/
David Crowder	CCM/Americana	http://crowdermusic.com
Gungor	CCM/Americana	www.gungormusic.com
Sojourn Music	CCM/Americana	http://sojournmusic.com/music
Voices As One	CCM/Catholic	http://voicesasone.com
Jesus Culture	CCM/Charismatic	http://jesusculture.com

Artist/Movement	Style	Website
Christ for the Nations	CCM/Missions	http://cfnmusic.com
Bethel	CCM/Youth	http://bethelmusic.com
Elevation Worship	CCM/Youth	http://elevationworship.com
Planet Shakers	CCM/Youth	www2.planetshakers.com/music
Iona/Wild Goose	Celtic	www.ionabooks.com/song-audio.html
Taizé	Contemplative/Liturgical	www.taize.fr/en_rubrique2603.html
Indelible Grace	Hymns/Americana	http://hymnbook.igracemusic.com
Cardiphonia	Hymns/Americana	http://cardiphonia.org
Oramos Cantando	Bilingual Hymns	
Aaron Niequist	Modern Hymns	www.aaronniequist.com
Hymns of the People	Modern Hymns	www.hymnsofthepeople.com
Keith and Kristyn Getty	Modern Hymns	www.gettymusic.com
Lift Up Your Hearts	Traditional Hymns	www.liftupyourheartshymnal.org
Hymns II	Traditional Hymns	
Salvador	Latino	www.salvadorlive.com
Christine D'Clario	Latino CCM	www.christinedclario.com
Danilo Montero	Latino CCM	http://danilomontero.net
Julissa	Latino CCM	www.weareworship.com/us/writers/julissa
Marco Barrientos	Latino CCM	http://marcobarrientos.com
Marcos Witt	Latino CCM	www.facebook.com/marcoswitt
Ingrid Rosario	Latino CCM/Gospel	www.ingridrosario.com
Joann Rosario	Latino CCM/Gospel	https://itunes.apple.com/us/artist/joann-rosario/id3830904
Joel Sierra	Latino Folk	https://www.facebook.com/pages/Joel-Sierra-Musica/349497128417344
Santiago Benavides	Latino Folk	http://santiagobenavides.com
Ricardo Sanchez	Latino/Gospel	http://ricardomusic.com

Appendix D

ORDER OF SERVICE EXAMPLES

ORDER OF SERVICE: CITY CHURCH (URBAN, MULTIETHNIC, PREDOMINATELY WHITE AND ASIAN, MILLENIALS)

10:00 Call to Worship: Read Psalm

10:01 Songs of Praise: Led by Sarah (Chinese American woman)

        1. Gospel medium-tempo song

        2. Latino upbeat song

        3. CCM medium-tempo song

10:16 Prayer of Invocation

10:17 Worship: Led by Tasha (African American woman)

        1. Gospel-infused CCM ballad

        2. Slow Gospel chorus

10:27 Closing Prayer

10:28 Greeting

10:30 Announcements

10:32 Offertory: Ensemble traditional hymn

10:35 Sermon on Acts 24:22–25:22

11:30 Benediction: Given by pastor

ORDER OF SERVICE: COMMUNITY CHURCH (URBAN, MULTIETHNIC, PREDOMINANTLY LATINO, MULTIGENERATIONAL)

9:30   Free Prayer (Pre-service)

   1. Free prayer and ad-libbed song (lasting 14 minutes)

   2. Invitation to prayer at altar

   3. Prayers of lament and hope and ad-libbed song

10:00   Songs of Praise

   1. Latin-infused CCM/Pentecostal song

   2. Latin-infused CCM/Pentecostal song

   3. Greeting (lasting 5 minutes)

   4. Gospel upbeat song

   5. Latin-infused gospel chorus

10:45   Sermon: By Pastor

11:45   Prayer Ministry: By Pastor

12:00   Church Ends

ORDER OF SERVICE: CALVIN SYMPOSIUM ON WORSHIP SERVICE, JANUARY 25, 2013, 4 TO 5 P.M.

Blessed Are the Persecuted: Worshiping in Solidarity with the Persecuted Church

"Revelation Song," by Jennie Lee Riddle (English, Korean, Spanish) (Explain the theme of service, then read Matthew 5:10: "Blessed are those who are persecuted for righteousness' sake, for theirs is the kingdom of heaven" [NRSV]. Each time a Scripture is read, the congregation responds with the following: "Blessed are the persecuted, for theirs is the kingdom of heaven.")

Read Matthew 5:10
"Blessed are the persecuted, for theirs is the kingdom of heaven."

Today we worship with our brothers and sisters in **Colombia**. According to some, Colombia is currently more unstable than it has been in the last thirty years. Guerrillas have openly committed murders in public streets and on buses. However, Christianity continues to grow in the country, and Marxist guerrillas and right-wing paramilitary groups see Christians as a threat to their recruitment of young men and women. In the last five years, Marxist guerrilla groups have killed more than three hundred evangelicals, mainly leaders, and displaced hundreds.
"Mi Vida Entera," by Santiago Benavides Cardenas (Aldaba) (Spanish, English)

Read James 1:2-4
"Blessed are the persecuted, for theirs is the kingdom of heaven."

Today we worship with our brothers and sisters in **Ethiopia**. During the Marxist years in Ethiopia (1974–1991), many of the churches in Ethiopia went underground for survival. And out of this underground church have come many powerful songs. Prominent among the many songwriters, Tesfaye Gabbiso was incarcerated for seven years because of his songs and public faith. Thus the songs became even more powerful. They were played on cassettes throughout both Christian and Muslim music shops, public markets and homes. "I Refuse, I Refrain" is one of Tesfaye's songs and is the testimony of the young men in the story of Nebuchadnezzar and the fiery furnace.
"I Refuse, I Refrain with Eyesus" (English, Amharic)

Read 1 Peter 1:6-7
"Blessed are the persecuted, for theirs is the kingdom of heaven."

Today we worship with our brothers and sisters in **Sudan**. In northern Sudan, the Interim National Constitution guarantees religious freedom, but Islam remains the de facto state religion. Muslims are given preferential treatment, and non-Islamic proselytism is prohibited. It is difficult for Christians to obtain permission to build churches. Converts face social pressure and harassment from security services. They typically do not stay in Sudan. The government knows that forcing hundreds of thousands of "southerners" to move to South Sudan will exacerbate humanitarian crises on both sides of the border. Those forced into South Sudan will have few resources to enable their return to an agricultural lifestyle; South Sudan already struggles to feed its own population. The climate for followers of Christianity has deteriorated since secession by the South. There has been a marked increase in threats and attacks against churches, priests and Christians of all denominations. "Baba al Fi Sama" (Arabic, Ki-swahili, English)

Read 1 Peter 5:8-9
"Blessed are the persecuted, for theirs is the kingdom of heaven."

Today we worship with our brothers and sisters in **Indonesia**. [Share a personal story about persecution.]
"O Lord, Our God/Ya, Tuhanku (Indonesian, English)

Read Psalm 23:4-5
"Blessed are the persecuted, for theirs is the kingdom of heaven."

Today we worship with our brothers and sisters in **India**. Violence against Christians continues at an alarming rate. Persecution comes in the form of beatings, murders, imprisonments, church demolitions, destruction of property and Bible burnings. Perpetrators are rarely charged with these crimes. Most of the violence is initiated by the thirty Hindu nationalist organizations that subscribe to an extremist ideology called Hindutva, which advocates the expulsion of non-Hindus from India. Six Indian states have laws against coerced religious conversion that are often used against Christians. The "anti-conversion" laws impose prison terms and hefty fines on anyone who converts Indians by force, fraud or allurement. On March 28, 2011, sixteen new Christian converts were arrested in Odisha (formerly Orissa) state for converting to Christianity without a permit.

"Bhaj Pavantam" (Hindi, English)

Read Psalm 30:9-12
"Blessed are the persecuted, for theirs is the kingdom of heaven."

Today we worship with our brothers and sisters in **Burma**. In Burma (officially known as Myanmar), authorities have perpetrated numerous human rights violations, including forced labor, genocides, rapes, tortures and detentions, mostly on Christian groups. In the last two years, the military has closed churches, imprisoned pastors, forced Christian children to work and offered money and promotions to soldiers who convert Christians to Buddhism. Christian minority groups, particularly the Karen and Chin groups, are singled out because of the government's goal to create a uniform society of one language, one ethnicity and one religion.

"How Great Thou Art" (English, Arabic, Chin)
"Blessed are the persecuted, for theirs is the kingdom of heaven."

Prayer (from the Book of Common Prayer): "Almighty God who created us in your own image: grant us grace fearlessly to contend against evil and to make no peace with oppression; and, that we may reverently use our freedom, help us to employ it in the maintenance of justice in our communities and among the nations, to the glory of your holy Name; through Jesus Christ our Lord, who lives and reigns with you and the Holy Spirit, one God, now and for ever. Amen."

(This service was led by members of the International Council of Ethnodoxologists: Robin Harris, Sandra Van Opstal, Josh Davis,

Appendix E

COMPONENTS OF WORSHIP

Gathering	Call to Worship ↓ Greeting ↓ Prayer of Adoration or Prayer of Invocation ↑ Call to Confession ↓ Prayer of Confession and Lament ↑ ↔ Assurance of Pardon ↓ Passing of the Peace ↓ ↔ Thanksgiving ↑ The Law ↓ Dedication ↑ ↔
Proclamation	Prayer for Illumination ↑ Scripture Reading ↓ Sermon ↓
Response to the Word	Profession of the Church's Faith ↑ Prayers of the People ↑ Offering ↑
The Lord's Supper	Declaration of God's Promises and Invitation ↓ Prayer of Thanksgiving ↑ Breaking of the Bread ↓ Communion ↓ ↔ Response of Thanksgiving ↑
Sending	Call to Service or Discipleship ↓ Blessing/Benediction ↓

This chart is useful for worship and can be used in any cultural setting as a way to think beyond style to content and form. It can also be used to make observations of worship cultures that are less familiar. It emphasizes the conversational reality of worship. The arrows indicate directions in which the conversation flows: from God to the people, from the people to God and among the people.

Adapted from Carrie Steenwyk and John D. Witvliet, *The Worship Sourcebook*, 2nd ed. (Grand Rapids: The Calvin Institute of Christian Worship / Faith Alive, 2013), 25; http://worship.calvin.edu/resources/publications/the-worship-sourcebook.

Appendix F

WORLD ASSEMBLY INTERNATIONAL CONFERENCE SONGS

The International Fellowship of Evangelical Students World Assembly is a gathering of global leaders from eighty different countries that meets every four years to gain vision for their movement around the world. It is hosted by a different continent each time, and the 2015 gathering was in Mexico. The song package used reflects the official languages of the gathering: English, Spanish and French (Canada, France and Francophone Africa). (Song usage represented: English 30%, Spanish 30%, multilingual 15%, French 10%, language of key speakers 15%.)

Table F.1

Song Title	Language
All Around/Again I Say Rejoice	English
Avec des Cris de Joie (With Shouts of Joy)	French
Be Like Him	Zulu
Canto de los Líderes (Leaders' Song)	Spanish
Con Mis Manos (With My Hands)	Spanish

Song Title	Language
De Todas as Tribos (From All the Nations)	Portuguese
Dieu Tu Puissant (How Great Thou Art)	French
Great Is Thy Faithfulness	Multilingual
Hakuna Mungu Kama (There's No One)	Swahili
Here I Am to Worship	English
Holy Spirit You Are Welcome	English
Holy, Holy, Holy, Lord God Almighty	Multilingual (English/Spanish/Portuguese/French)
How Great Is Our God	Multilingual (English/Spanish/French/Portuguese)
Il M'a Sauve (He Saved Me)	French Creole
In Christ Alone	English
Magdan Lik (Glory to You)	Arabic
May the Mind of Christ	English
Mi Vida Entera (My Whole Life)	Spanish
Nee Matram Mathi	Malyalam
No Other Name	Multilingual (English/Korean)
O for a Thousand Tongues	English
Open the Eyes (Holy)	Multilingual (English/Spanish/French)
Revelation Song	Multilingual (English/Spanish/French/Mandarin)
Siyabonga Jesu (Thank You Jesus)	Kiswati
Tenemos Esperanza (We Have Hope)	Spanish
Yeshu Terra Naam (Jesus Your Name Is Higher)	Hindi
Yesu Azali Awa (Jesus Christ Is with Us)	Congolese
Yo Soy Militante (I Am a Militant)	Spanish
Your Great Name	English

Appendix G

SONGS FOR CROSSING CULTURES

Table G.1

Songs by Culture	Style	Artist/Language
Latino		
Noy Hadie Como Tu (No One Like You)	slow	Marco Barrientos
Nombre No Hay (No Other Name)	upbeat	Freddy Rodriquez
Eres Todo Poderoso (You Are All Powerful)	rock	Rojo
Montāna (Mountain)	upbeat	Salvador
Gospel		
Say So	upbeat	Israel Houghton
Praise the Lord with Me	medium tempo	Bishop T. D. Jakes
I Give Myself Away	slow	William McDowell
Freedom	upbeat	Eddie James
CCM		
How Great Is Our God	medium tempo	Chris Tomlin, Passion
The Stand	medium tempo	Hillsong United
Revelation Song	slow	Kari Jobe
How He Loves	slow	Kim Walker, Jesus Culture

Songs by Culture	Style	Artist/Language
Crossover Hymns (style and language depend on your goal for the song)		
Great Is Thy Faithfulness		
Amazing Grace		
I Surrender All		
Oh How I Love Jesus		
Global (from Urbana 09 and 12)		
Magdan Lik (Glory to You)	upbeat	Arabic (Egypt)
Hakuna Mungu Kama Wewe (There's No One Like Jesus)	upbeat	Kiswahili (Kenya)
Yesu Azali Awa (Jesus Christ Is with Us)	medium tempo	Congolese (Congo)
Yeshu Terra Naam (Jesus, Your Name Is Higher)	medium tempo	Hindi (India)

Appendix H

TEACHING A LANGUAGE SONG

1. Learn it first. As the leader you must be able to pronounce the words of the song before you teach it to your team and congregation. Ideally learn it from a native speaker and have them confirm the spelling and translation you will use.

2. Songs should make sense for your context (see "Gathering the Right Ingredients" in chapter 6).

3. Choose songs that have easier words to sing, ideally short choruses with repeating words. It is best that a native speaker consult with someone who is completely unfamiliar with the language. Then choose a series of songs with shared words. If the song is particularly hard, sing the verses and have the congregation join you on the chorus.

4. Sing the pronunciation from the beginning instead of speaking. It is easier to learn words to music. (If the song has an English version, teach that first.)

5. Teach the song line by line and have the congregation repeat after you. Sing in a really slow tempo, accompanied only by one instrument. Watch them to see if they are catching on.

6. When you feel confident, sing phrase by phrase together

through the entire section. You may want to repeat each phrase two times, and then the section two times.

7. When there are words or rhythms that are hard to get, repeat that section over and over until it flows. It helps to stay on a phrase and sing and move if it's particularly difficult. Moving their bodies will help.

8. Pastor them. Encourage them in their risk taking and free them to make mistakes. Explain to them that you are singing as an act of both hospitality and solidarity. Remind them of what the song means and share something personally meaningful about it.

9. Sing at full tempo and encourage them to sing the parts they are able to catch.

10. Teach the song as a prelude to worship. Lead the beginning of the set. Then, sing the song again at the end of the set or at least in the next set. (If you are teaching multiple language songs try to add one in each set or each week instead of teaching them all in one set. You can also stick to songs of one language per set that share words.)

11. Absolutely make sure you have the translations on PowerPoint.

Appendix I

WORSHIP CULTURES

These descriptions were developed originally as a team dialogue from our experiences with the Urbana 03 worship team (with contributions from Krista-Dawn Kimsey, Paul Chin, James Choung, Matt Ryan Kelzenberg, Corey Saffold, Erna Stubblefield, Todd Waldo and Sandra Van Opstal). Over a decade, dozens of worship leaders from diverse backgrounds who have led crossculturally have contributed to the dialogue. This is a reflection from our own personal experiences, reading and observations. Please do not use these to stereotype; these are archetypes. Each style has an incredible breadth of diversity within it as you overlay denomination and theology. Since Native Americans were absent from our team, we did not want to take it upon ourselves to interpret Native worship styles. Great resources are available from Mark Charles (Navajo) at the Calvin Institute of Christian Worship website (http://worship.calvin.edu/about/staff-directory /mark-charles).

Congregational worship in African American, Asian American, Latino and White (Western influenced) communities can be thought of in the categories of overall themes and atmosphere, role of the worship leader, and distinct musical elements.

OVERALL THEMES AND ATMOSPHERE

We sing and talk about the characteristics of God that are important to us based on our experiences. The themes that are emphasized in a church come from the narrative of a particular worshiping community.

African American worship is an experience of freedom and remembrance of God's power. His promises are a deep source of joy. There are songs and prayers of remembering God's faithfulness throughout history. Worship therefore is an opportunity to experience this freedom now and to hope for the deliverance God will bring to the oppressed. This freedom is for the individual worshipers as they express emotion outwardly, and for the community with spontaneity in the service.

Asian American worship is an intimate moment of devotion with God. Sacrifice and servanthood are ultimate Asian cultural expressions of love; consequently, many songs focus on total service and devotion in response to God's sacrifice of his Son. God's glory and holiness inspire deep awe and reverence, while a connection with a close and tender Father brings healing. Worship is a quiet intensity that is not necessarily outwardly expressed as intensely as it is felt. Worship provides an escape from the expectations of community and gives an opportunity to seek individual expression.

Latino worship is a communal celebration of the presence of the Holy Spirit. Joy is experienced as the community anticipates and expects God to do something. There is often space within the worship time to wait on the Lord and unload your burdens. In community, there is permission for people to have outward (and audible) expressions of deep emotion (crying or shouting) during the worship service. It is a Spirit-filled fiesta celebrating the goodness of God.

White/Western worship is intentional adoration of a triune God. Worship is often intentionally structured to form our understanding of God. A personal relationship with God our Father is often sung about. The cross and God's sacrifice for us through his Son Jesus and our response of repentance and forgiveness are also common themes. Standing with the broader church, specifically the historical church through prayers, liturgy and hymns, is important. Creation and nature are commonly reasons to give praise.

THE ROLE OF THE LEADER

Beyond singing and playing certain styles of music, it is important to know what the job of the leader is within that community. Each community may be given a key word to describe that role.

African American: exhortation. The leader passionately exhorts the congregation to worship God with their whole being. Often described as being "anointed" by God to take spiritual authority, leaders direct the congregation to worship as they feel the Holy Spirit leading them. They create energy and momentum in the group. For example, the leader may say to the congregation, "Tell the person next to you that God is here."

Asian American: invitation. Leadership is demonstrated humbly by being an authentic lead worshiper. The leader is focused on her own worship experience, relying on her example to give instruction and space for others to worship. Too much speaking could be interpreted as a sign that the worship leader is not fully worshiping. Musical dynamics are used as nonverbal cues, reflecting the cultural value of indirect communication. The congregation waits for an invitation to "enter in" collectively.

Latino: interpretation. The leader interprets what the Holy Spirit is doing in the community. For example, the leader may say to the congregation, "I can tell the Spirit is thick in this place." Leaders help create and lead a communal experience of worshiping God. The worship leader will call out to the congregation and invite a response, whether in singing or shouting praise. The leader will be interacting with the congregation.

White/Western: explanation. The leader teaches the congregation about who God is and how we should appropriately respond to him. Often the leader will offer an explanation before the song so that the content is well apprehended. This can either be Scripture or a personal story. The congregation will follow the vocal lines and posture of the leader, so the leader can give permission to the congregation to respond in a variety of ways.

DISTINCT MUSICAL ELEMENTS

Music selection, instrumentation, volume levels and length of time play out in distinct ways within cultural contexts. You may hear the same song in different cultures and not recognize it.

African American worship encompasses many different genres of music including mass choir, gospel, hymns and rock crossover. Repetition is the most common musical element in African American worship. The reason for the repetition is to give the "whole person" a chance to respond to the truth of the words. The core band instruments are keyboard, bass and drums, but the focus is the vocals. Doing things together like complicated harmonies, solo improvisations and choral swells creates that tight sound. The leader often ad-libs and rarely sings the words of the song—that is the job of the choir or the vocal team. The congregation is free to clap, dance, sing harmony and respond to the Holy Spirit however they wish. People typically clap on beats two and four. "Having church" happens only when worship has sufficiently allowed for an emotional interchange between the individual and the Holy Spirit. Since this cannot be planned, space must be created. A song can extend for fifteen minutes in order to allow for spontaneous response to the Spirit.

Asian American worship can initially sound like CCM since

songs from worship movements such as Hillsong and Passion are sung, but in reality two things set it apart: the song themes and the space created. The musicians on the team are typically competent and could mimic any style of music, but instrumentalists don't want to attract too much attention to themselves by playing complicated solos because that would detract attention from worshiping God. Clean and absent of complications describes both the instrumentation (small band) and the vocals (lead, one extra melody and one harmony). Musical dynamics are very important, though much more subtle. The soft, more intimate times are very quiet, while the loud times are not as spontaneous or exuberant as other cultural expressions. There needs to be enough time for worship to build in intensity but also to create quiet space for intimacy; this often feels like a roller coaster. A common musical tag is to end the song by slowing the tempo considerably and repeating the chorus out of tempo. This allows for one last opportunity to reflect on the content of the song.

Latino worship encompasses many different genres of music including modern rock, classic salsa and reggae. The differences in style of music are often rooted in generational preferences. The rhythm section is important. Auxiliary percussion, tambourines, congas and the drums are essential instruments for some (Caribbean). In other settings (Mexican and Central American), multiple guitars are needed. Clapping happens on every beat. Vocal harmonization is not fancy; often you can find six singers on the melody. Language is also an important factor in Latino congregations: some are English speaking, some Spanish dominant and others bilingual (even Spanglish). Latino worship is not synonymous with singing in Spanish. Songs often repeat themselves and increase in intensity as they do. The volume levels of worship are loud and louder—giving people permission to express themselves boldly. Meditative worship is still loud. Worship is not declared

done by the clock, but by the congregation's experience with the
Holy Spirit. The service is over when the entire congregation has
met with the Lord (unless the Blackhawks are playing).

White/Western worship encompasses many different genres of
music including modern rock, hymns and folk. It is as diverse as
African American, Asian or Latino genres. Whether hymns and
organ, rock band or mandolins, planning is important. Songs are
often done in a similar way every time. There may be some repetition involved, but it is usually planned out by the band ahead of
time, and the general order of the song rarely changes. Often the
chorus will be repeated and the last line of the song repeated as an
ending tag. In order for everyone to sing the right words together,
there is almost always a hymnal, chorus book or PowerPoint pro-
jection of the words. The leader sings the exact words and rarely
ad-libs. If there is clapping, it happens on beats one and three. The
volume usually depends on the generations represented in the
church; people do, however, like to hear themselves sing. The time
can be short or long depending on what has been planned.

It might be helpful to look at good articles about worship music
and ask questions about which values are essential and which are
preferences that are culturally located. For example, see Ed Stetzer,
"A Letter to My Worship Leaders" (parts 1 and 2), *The Exchange*
(blog), www.christianitytoday.com/edstetzer/2014/november
/letter-to-my-worship-leaders-part-1.html; www.christianitytoday
.com/edstetzer/2014/november/letter-to-my-worship-leaders
-part-2.html.

NOTES

INTRODUCTION

[1]Alison Siewert, conversation with the author, April 25, 2015.

[2]Monique Ingalls, "Spiritual Journeys in Evangelical Conference Worship," *Ethnomusicology*, Spring-Summer 2011, 261-62.

[3]The Hmong are an ethnic group from the mountainous regions of Southeast Asia.

[4]Justo L. González, *¡Alabadle! Hispanic Christian Worship* (Nashville: Abingdon Press, 1996), 19.

[5]Pedrito U. Maynard-Reid, *Diverse Worship* (Downers Grove, IL: IVP Academic, 2009), 19.

[6]Richard J. Foster, *Celebration of Discipline* (New York: HarperOne, 1998), 158.

[7]Ron Man, "Blended Worship: Good for the Body," Calvin Symposium on Worship, Calvin College, January 24-26, 2008.

CHAPTER 1: TENSION AT THE TABLE

[1]See urbana.org/seminar/worship-urbana-why-does-it-look-way.

[2]"Table," in *Dictionary of Biblical Imagery*, ed. Leland Ryken, James C. Wilhoit and Tremper Longman III (Downers Grove, IL: InterVarsity Press, 1998), 841.

[3]"Meal," in Ryken, Wilhoit and Longman, *Dictionary of Biblical Imagery*, 544.

[4]I think they only come for the food because it's a night of the week they don't have to think about cooking.

[5]All recipes can be found at sandravanopstal.com.

[6]See James Emery White, *The Rise of the Nones* (Grand Rapids: Baker, 2014); and George Barna and David Kinnaman, *Churchless* (Carol Stream, IL: Tyndale Momentum, 2014).

[7]Pew Research Center, "'Nones' on the Rise," October 9, 2012, www.pew forum.org/2012/10/09/nones-on-the-rise.

[8]Ibid.

[9]Barna Group provides information on topics such as "Six Reasons Young Christians Leave Church" (www.barna.org/teens-next-gen-articles/528-six -reasons-young-christians-leave-church) and "Designing Worship Spaces with Millennials in Mind" (www.barna.org/barna-update/millennials/689 -designing-worship-spaces-with-millennials-in-mind#).

[10]Bob Smietana, "Are Millennials Really Leaving the Church? Yes—but Mostly White Millennials," On Faith, www.faithstreet.com/onfaith /2014/05/16/are-millennials-really-leaving-church-yes-but-mostly-white -millennials/32103.

[11]Pew Research Center, "'Nones' on the Rise."

[12]Smietana, "Are Millennials Really Leaving the Church?"

[13]A great library of resources on worship can be found at the Institute's website: http://worship.calvin.edu.

[14]These categories (transcultural, crosscultural, contextual, countercultural) are, in turn, adapted from the Nairobi Statement on Worship and Culture developed by the Lutheran World Federation.

[15]Andy Crouch, *Culture Making* (Downers Grove, IL: InterVarsity Press, 2008), 155.

[16]Robin P. Harris, "The Great Misconception: Why Music Is Not a Universal Language," in *Worship and Mission for the Global Church: An Ethnodoxology Handbook*, ed. James R. Krabill (Pasadena, CA: William Carey Library, 2012), 109.

Chapter 2: Is PB&J Ethnic Food?

[1]Paula Harris and Doug Schaupp, *Being White: Finding Our Place in a Multi-ethnic World* (Downers Grove, IL: InterVarsity Press, 2004), 103-4.

[2]COGIC is the acronym for Church of God in Christ, an African American Pentecostal denomination that parallels the Assemblies of God.

[3]Spencer Perkins, quoted in Joe Maxwell, "Obituary: Racial Reconciler Spencer Perkins," *Christianity Today*, March 2, 1998, www.christianitytoday .com/ct/1998/march2/8t3073.html.

[4]*The Oxford Pocket Dictionary of Current English*, s.v. "practice," Encyclopedia .com; *Merriam-Webster.com*, s.v. "discipline."

[5]John Witvliet, "Further Thoughts on Formative and Expressive Worship"

(lecture handout, Forming Worshipping Communities class, Calvin Theological Seminary, Grand Rapids, MI, fall 2014).

[6]See my book *The Mission of Worship* (Downers Grove, IL: InterVarsity Press, 2012).

[7]The Brookings Institution report shows the rise of Hispanics, projected to make up 25.1 percent of the US population in 2044. The African American percentage will be half that. William H. Frey, "New Projections Point to a Majority Minority Nation in 2044," Brookings, December 12, 2014, www.brookings.edu/blogs/the-avenue/posts/2014/12/12-majority -minority-nation-2044-frey?utm_campaign=Brookings+Brief&utm _source=hs_.

[8]Michael O. Emerson, "A New Day for Multiracial Congregations," Yale University *Reflections*, Spring 2013, http://reflections.yale.edu/article/future -race/new-day-multiracial-congregations. Emerson cites the 2010 National Survey of Congregations by Faith Communities Today.

[9]Scott Thumma, "Racial Diversity Increasing in U.S. Congregations," *Huffington Post*, March 24, 2013, www.huffingtonpost.com/scott-thumma-phd /racial-diversity-increasing-in-us-congregations_b_2944470.html.

[10]The 20 percent figure comes from the 2012 National Congregations Study; Michael Lipka, "Many U.S. Congregations Are Still Racially Segregated, but Things Are Changing," December 8, 2014, Pew Research Center, www .pewresearch.org/fact-tank/2014/12/08/many-u-s-congregations-are-still -racially-segregated-but-things-are-changing-2.

[11]Emerson, "A New Day for Multiracial Congregations."

[12]Terry W. York, "Multicultural Congregations and Worship: A Literature Review," *Journal of Family and Community Ministries* 27 (2014): 1.

CHAPTER 3: FOOD FIGHTS

[1]The tradition of the bride and groom jumping the broom was developed by the African American slave community as a symbol of marriage between two people who, based on the laws at the time, could not be legally wed.

[2]As part of the ceremony to symbolize unity a lasso (cord) is placed around the couple after they have exchanged their vows. It is symbolic of their love, which should bind them together as they equally share the responsibility of marriage for the rest of their lives.

[3]In Spanish-influenced cultures *las arras* are thirteen coins that are given by

the bride to the groom, traditionally as a dowry, or from the groom to the bride as a symbol of his commitment to care for her and her acceptance of them as a sign of her trust he will do so.

[4]The dollar dance is a Polish tradition from the early 1900s that encourages wedding guests to dance briefly with either the bride or groom while offering cash as a payment, often pinned to the clothes or collected by a close family or friend.

[5]Kenneth E. Bailey, *Jesus Through Middle Eastern Eyes* (Downers Grove, IL: IVP Academic, 2008), 319.

[6]"Banquet," in *Dictionary of Biblical Imagery*, ed. Leland Ryken, James C. Wilhoit and Tremper Longman III (Downers Grove, IL: InterVarsity Press, 1998).

[7]Kenneth E. Bailey, *Poet & Peasant and Through Peasant Eyes* (Grand Rapids: Eerdmans, 1983), 98-99.

[8]Bailey, *Jesus Through Middle Eastern Eyes*, 315-16.

[9]Ibid., 315.

[10]"Table," in *Dictionary of Biblical Imagery*, 841.

[11]The term *Eucharist* means thanksgiving and was referred to as that by the by an early church discipleship document called the Didache (late first or early second century).

[12]Justo González, *The Story Luke Tells: Luke's Unique Witness to the Gospel* (Grand Rapids: Eerdmans, 2015), 94-95.

[13]Ibid., 95.

[14]Brenda Salter McNeil and Rick Richardson, *The Heart of Racial Justice: How Soul Change Leads to Social Change* (Downers Grove, IL: InterVarsity Press, 2004), 61-62.

[15]David Briggs, "Racial Power vs. Divine Glory: Why Desegregation Remains an Elusive Goal for U.S. Congregations," *ARDA*, February 28, 2014, http://blogs.thearda.com/trend/featured/racial-power-vs-divine-glory -why-desegregation-remains-an-elusive-goal-for-u-s-congregations.

[16]Ibid.

[17]Later, we will explore the concept of host-guest mentality in diverse worship and which models may help to stay away from abuse of power.

[18]"Aleluya, Aleluya, Mi alabanza sube a Ti" means "Hallelujah, Hallelujah, My praise rises to you." It comes from "Mi Alabanza Seguira," written by Edwin Santiago. The song can be heard at www.youtube.com/watch?v =3v6aHfahVZQ. See also www.youtube.com/watch?v=CcgYeFFpaog.

[19]Rev. Dr. Liz Mosbo VerHage, pastor of global and local ministries at Quest Church, provided this story.

[20]Watch a video of "Magdan Lik" sung at Urbana 09 at https://vimeo .com/9707504.

[21]*Christianity Today* has "noted the growing gap in how black and white Christians think about race since 2006, including [which group] thinks 'separate but equal' is sufficient and who wants to stop talking about race altogether. In its own examination of data from the 2012 General Social Survey, CT found that, on several race-related variables, there was no distinguishable difference between the general population and evangelicals who attend church at least once a week. Churchgoing evangelicals are not significantly different from the average American on race issues, including the likelihood of: being close friends with a white or black person; thinking blacks should be able to 'overcome prejudice and work their way up;' thinking the government should offer race-based special treatment; or supporting affirmative action hiring preferences." Ruth Moon, "Does the Gospel Mandate Racial Reconciliation? White Pastors Agree More Than Black Pastors," *Christianity Today*, December 16, 2014, www.christianitytoday.com/gleanings/2014 /december/does-gospel-mandate-racial-reconciliation-lifeway-kainos.html.

[22]Shannon Jammal-Hollemans, "Reconciliation Breaking Through: The Miracle of Reconciliation," Christian Reformed Church in North America Advent devotional, December 1, 2014, http://www2.crcna.org/pages/osj _adventdevotions.cfm.

[23]Views on racial relations are becoming increasingly polarized in evangelical communities. When asked about the statement "One of the most effective ways to improve race relations is to stop talking about race," in 2006 51 percent of whites and 24 percent of blacks agreed. In 2012 69 percent of whites and 34 percent of blacks agreed. In six years we increasingly believe the less we talk about race relations the better it will be, which is the opposite of what black Christian leaders are asking for. See Morgan Lee, "Behind Ferguson: How Black and White Christians Think Differently About Race," *Christianity Today*, August 21, 2014, www.christianitytoday .com/gleanings/2014/august/behind-ferguson-how-black-and-white -christians-think-race.html.

[24]Christian colleges are overwhelmingly white, and generally less diverse than their secular counterparts, which is something in itself to be lamented.

[25]Mime troupes are very common in African American and Latino urban

churches. Mime is a way to use dance and music to express what words cannot. It is also used with youth (such as my upstairs neighbors) as a way to give them an outlet to express themselves.

[26]For an idea of why this was so offensive, do an Internet search on blackface. Imagine a white student asking if black students in mime were whiteface.

CHAPTER 4: HOSTING WELL

[1]David Joachim, *A Man, a Can, a Plan* (Emmaus, PA: Rodale Books, 2002).

[2]Terry W. York, "Multicultural Congregations and Worship: A Literature Review," *Journal of Family and Community Ministries* 27 (2014): 1.

[3]James E. Plueddemann, *Leading Across Cultures: Effective Ministry and Mission in the Global Church* (Downers Grove, IL: IVP Academic, 2009), 161.

[4]Personal correspondence with the author.

[5]Plueddemann, *Leading Across Cultures*, 153.

[6]Ibid., 155.

[7]For a great book on gender and leadership see Sheryl Sandberg, *Lean In: Women, Work, and the Will to Lead* (New York: Knopf, 2013).

[8]Paul Tokunaga, *Invitation to Lead: Guidance for Emerging Asian American Leaders* (Downers Grove, IL: InterVarsity Press, 2003), 59.

[9]Ibid., 54.

[10]This information was gathered from a lecture in the class "Forming Worshipping Communities," Calvin Seminary, fall 2014.

[11]Personal communication with the author.

CHAPTER 5: DESIGNING YOUR MENU

[1]Soong-Chan Rah, *The Next Evangelicalism: Freeing the Church from Western Cultural Captivity* (Downers Grove, IL: InterVarsity Press, 2009), 86.

[2]Sriracha is a red chili-based Asian hot sauce.

[3]Israel Houghton, "I Hear the Sound," from the album *Live from Another Level*, Integrity Music, 2004.

[4]The concert-and-sermon approach is a form of worship in which there is an opening song, four worship songs, ad-libbed prayers, the sermon and announcements. It is a form of liturgy.

[5]When music producers wanted huge sales for albums recorded by black artists, they changed the musicians' style to appeal to the white audience. The same goes for Latinos such as Gloria Estefan and Enrique Iglesias.

With the worship music industry being similarly produced, I wonder if fusion is doing the same with Christian artists of color.

[6]Monique Ingalls, phone interview with the author, January 16, 2013, and email, May 11, 2015.

[7]George Yancey, *One Body, One Spirit: Principles of Successful Multiethnic Churches* (Downers Grove, IL: InterVarsity Press, 2003); Curtiss Paul DeYoung, Michael O. Emerson, George Yancey and Karen Chai Kim, *United by Faith: The Multiracial Congregation as an Answer to the Problem of Race* (New York: Oxford University Press, 2004).

[8]Gerardo Marti, *Worship Across the Racial Divide* (New York: Oxford University Press, 2012), 1.

[9]Ibid., 16-22.

[10]Ibid., 17, 19.

[11]Ibid., 81-83.

[12]More information on Marti's research on "practice based approach" can be found in ibid., 15-22, 180-96, 199-212.

[13]Andrés T. Tapia, *The Inclusion Paradox*, 2nd ed. (n.p.: Andrés T. Tapia, 2013), 99-100.

[14]Appalachian music fuses ballads from England, Ireland and Scotland with a Scots fiddle and the banjo, an instrument popularized by African American slaves in the eighteenth century. Blues music has similar roots. See "Appalachian Music," https://en.wikipedia.org/wiki/Appalachian_music.

[15]Katelin Hansen, personal conversation, February 15, 2015.

CHAPTER 6: IT'S NOT JUST THE FOOD

[1]Russell Yee, *Worship on the Way: Exploring Asian North American Christian Experience* (Valley Forge: Judson, 2012), 7.

[2]Sandra Van Opstal, *The Mission of Worship* (Downers Grove, IL: InterVarsity Press, 2012), 17. Chandler's points are found in Paul-Gordon Chandler, *God's Global Mosaic* (Downers Grove, IL: InterVarsity Press, 1996), 16-17.

[3]Edward T. Hall developed the iceberg analogy of culture, which states that visible behaviors only account for 10 percent of the iceberg. The other 90 percent are beliefs and values.

[4]Robert E. Webber, *Worship Old and New*, rev. ed. (Grand Rapids: Zondervan, 1994), 149-51.

[5]Joan elaborates on this by referencing the reflections of Darrell Harris (Star

Song Records) and Chuck Fromm (*Worship Leader* magazine). Joan Huyser-Honig, "Robert E. Webber's Legacy: Ancient Future Faith and Worship," Calvin Institute of Christian Worship, May 18, 2007, http://worship.calvin .edu/resources/resource-library/robert-e-webber-s-legacy-ancient-future -faith-and-worship.

[6]Homogeneous worship would be offensive, but I have experienced this many times. Typically a US-led ministry assimilates a global gathering into North American worship. Truly international movements should work harder to provide spaces that reflect the diversity of their global ministry.

[7]*Urban* is often understood to mean African American. In reality it could also be Latino, Southeast Asian or some combination of the three.

[8]Each community has many different expressions within it. For example, black gospel services have spirituals, mass choir songs, rhythm and blues, urban contemporary, hip-hop, CCM, fusion and others.

[9]Mashup is the practice of putting two songs together (aka a medley).

[10]For more information on Melissa Vallejo, visit her website at http://www .melissavallejo.com.

[11]A full chart of components and movement can be found in appendix E.

[12]Mark Charles, "Contextualizing Worship: My Journey to Worship God as a Navajo Christian," Calvin Symposium on Worship, January 1, 2009, http://worship.calvin.edu/resources/resource-library/contextualizing -worship-my-journey-to-worship-god-as-a-navajo-christian/.

[13]Table 6.3 is based on information found at Mark Charles, "Time Perception Among Navajo American Indians and Its Relation to Academic Success," *Wirelessshogan*, August 2011, http://wirelesshogan.com/key_issues/navajo _time_perception.

[14]Charles, "Contextualizing Worship."

[15]John Witvliet, lecture in "Forming Worshipping Communities," Calvin Seminary, fall 2014.

[16]*Whiplash* is a term I like to use to describe moving so quickly from one genre and style to another that the congregation feels thrown around.

[17]An interesting study about relational interactions in worship services is found in Laura Meckler, "How Churches Are Slowly Becoming Less Segregated: Pastors Seeking Racially Diverse Congregations Cope with Culture Clashes; Should Children Be Shushed?," *Wall Street Journal*, October 13, 2014, www.wsj.com/articles/a-church-of-many-colors-the-most-segregated

-hour-in-america-gets-less-so-1413253801. The latest issue in our congregation was whether it is appropriate for women to breastfeed in the worship service or whether they should be escorted to the nursing room.

[18]This Calvin Symposium 2013 Vespers service can be found at http://worship .calvin.edu/resources/resource-library/blessed-are-the-persecuted-worshiping -in-solidarity-with-the-suffering-church.

CHAPTER 7: GUESS WHO'S COMING TO DINNER

[1]Mark Charles, "Just as It Should Be," *Calvin Institute of Christian Worship*, June 1, 2009, worship.calvin.edu/resources/resource-library/just-as-it -should-be.

[2]Brad Harper and Paul Louis Metzger, "Here We Are to Worship: Six Principles That Might Bring a Truce to the Age-Old Tension Between Tradition and Popular Culture," *Christianity Today*, August 21, 2009, www.christianity today.com/ct/2009/august/31.32.html.

[3]Thabiti Anyabwile, "The Divide in the Black Church That Most Troubles Me," *The Front Porch*, July 1, 2014, http://thefrontporch.org/2014/07/the -divide-in-the-black-church-that-most-troubles-me.

[4]These steps are based on John Kotter's 8-Step Process. Though he proposes eight of them, I have focused on those I think are more helpful. Kotter International, "The 8-Step Process for Leading Change," www.kotterinter national.com/the-8-step-process-for-leading-change.

[5]"The Lord's Supper (1994)," Christian Reformed Church, accessed May 18, 2015, www.crcna.org/resources/church-resources/liturgical-forms-resources /lords-supper/lords-supper-1994.

[6]The negative response is due to a great divide that exists between Latino Catholics and Protestants, which is more pronounced than in completely white American contexts. Symbols and images from their previous experience as Catholics is off-putting.

[7]Makoto Fujimura, *Culture Care: Reconnecting with Beauty for Our Common Life* (New York: Fujimura Institute, 2014); quoted in Mark Beuving, "Book of the Month: Culture Care," *Theology for Real Life Faculty Blog*, December 29, 2014, http://facultyblog.eternitybiblecollege.com/2014/12/book-of-the -month-culture-care/#.Vaf84flnEUo.

[8]"Who We Are," *Proskuneo*, accessed May 18, 2015, www.proskuneo.org.

[9]"Worship Resources," *Arrabon*, accessed May 18, 2015, http://arrabon.com /worship-resources.

CHAPTER 8: MASTER CHEF

[1] For a brief description of ENFP see "The 16 MBTI® Types," *Myers and Briggs Foundation*, accessed May 18, 2015, www.myersbriggs.org/my-mbti -personality-type/mbti-basics/the-16-mbti-types.htm.

[2] Imagine what the editing process of this book was like for my loved ones.

[3] This model was developed by Daniel Goleman; the figure is adapted from "Emotional Intelligence Theory: Highlighting and Developing Leadership Skills," Educational Business Articles, accessed May 18, 2015, www.educational -business-articles.com/emotional-intelligence-theory.html.

[4] Andy Kim, Urbana blog (content no longer available online).

[5] See InterVarsity's "Diverse Worship Matters" videos at https://vimeo .com/119363874 (summary); https://vimeo.com/115291470 (video 1); https:// vimeo.com/116011233 (video 2); https://vimeo.com/117637951 (video 3).

[6] Justo González, *The Story Luke Tells: Luke's Unique Witness to the Gospel* (Grand Rapids: Eerdmans, 2015), 93.

[7] Ben Shin, phone conversation with the author, April 17, 2015.

[8] Audrey Tom, "On Stage: Check Your Egos at the Door," *Audrey Tom* (blog), January 9, 2015, https://moomooaudrey.wordpress.com/2013/01/09/the -stage-check-your-egos-at-the-door.

EPILOGUE: NORTH PARK UNIVERSITY

[1] Stephen Kelly, phone conversation with the author, April 23, 2015.

ABOUT THE AUTHOR

Sandra Van Opstal is a Chicago-born, second-generation Latina and a leading practitioner of multiethnic worship. A preacher, trainer, liturgist and activist, she is passionate about creating atmospheres that mobilize for reconciliation and justice. She served as the worship director for the Urbana Student Missions Conference, IFES World Assembly and Lausanne Younger Leader Gatherings and has led worship for the Willow Creek Association, the Christian Community Development Association, InterVarsity Christian Fellowship, the Evangelical Covenant Church and the Evangelical Immigration Table. She regularly consults as both a worship leader and a crosscultural trainer with Christian colleges, conferences and local churches, and she serves on the board of the Christian Community Development Association. She is a pastor at Grace and Peace Community in Chicago, and is the author of *The Mission of Worship*.

IVP PRAXIS

EQUIPPING LEADERS FOR MINISTRY

"...TO EQUIP HIS PEOPLE FOR WORKS OF SERVICE,
SO THAT THE BODY OF CHRIST MAY BE BUILT UP."

EPHESIANS 4:12

God has called us to ministry. But it's not enough to have a vision for ministry if you don't have the practical skills for it. Nor is it enough to do the work of ministry if what you do is headed in the wrong direction. We need both vision *and* expertise for effective ministry. We need *praxis*.

Praxis puts theory into practice. It brings cutting-edge ministry expertise from visionary practitioners. You'll find sound biblical and theological foundations for ministry in the real world, with concrete examples for effective action and pastoral ministry. Praxis books are more than the "how to"—they're also the "why to." And because *being* is every bit as important as *doing*, Praxis attends to the inner life of the leader as well as the outer work of ministry. Feed your soul, and feed your ministry.

If you are called to ministry, you know you can't do it on your own. Let Praxis provide the companions you need to equip God's people for life in the kingdom.

www.ivpress.com/praxis